WIKI GOD

WIKI GOD

THE DANGEROUS EDITABLE DEITY

TRAVIS AGNEW

WIKI GOD

Copyright © 2019 by Travis Agnew

Tag Publishing

All rights reserved.

Printed in the United States of America.

ISBN: 9781795506144

Scripture quotations are from The Holy Bible, English Standard Version © 2001 by Crossway Bibles, a publishing ministry of Good News Publishers. Used by permission. All rights reserved.

All rights reserved. No part of this publication may be reproduced, stored, in a retrieval system, or transmitted in any form or by any means - electronic, mechanical, photocopy, recording, or any other - except for brief quotations in printed reviews, without the prior permission of the publisher.

To Aiden,

Your voice finally gave me the permission to speak of God
in a way that my soul had always longed to proclaim.

TABLE OF CONTENTS

Preface	1
1: The Editable God	5
2: The Needy God	21
3: The Man Upstairs God	31
4: The Video Screen God	41
5: The Geriatric God	51
6: The Upgraded God	61
7: The Little Engine That Could God	71
8: The Overbooked God	81
9: The Undergraduate God	91
10: The Pollster God	101
11: The Permission-Seeking God	111
12: The Unreliable God	121
13: The Grade-on-a-Curve God	131
14: The Shady Past God	141
15: The Pushover God	151
16: The Thunderbolt God	161
17: The Fuddy-Duddy God	171
18: The Talent Judge God	181
19: The Chutes & Ladders God	191
20: The Buffet God	201
Scripture Index	217

PREFACE

My name is Travis Agnew. I am a disciple of Jesus Christ, a husband to Amanda, a father to the best kids in the world, a pastor who still loves the opportunity to make disciples within the local church, and a creative who loves to share resources through blog posts, podcasts, and books. And that's where we find ourselves today. You are holding in your hands a book concept that has been simmering in my soul for almost twenty years before it was finally released.

I began following Jesus when I was seven years old. Like every believer, I've had times of encouraging growth and times of glaring apathy. My story has significant milestones along the way that formed me into who I am. One such pivotal moments happened while listening to a sermon when I was in college. The preacher casually mentioned a quote from some guy named A.W. Tozer. I have no idea what he said afterward because my mind and heart were being undone as I wrestled with the quote's claims.

"What comes to your mind when you think about God is the most important thing about you." I wanted to object with the deceased Tozer, but I could not. Knowing God is my greatest pursuit. To understand him should be my highest priority. My theology will dictate my life. After the service that day, I searched out the writings of Tozer and was introduced to his teachings on the attributes of God. His lofty depictions of God infected my mind in the most glorious of ways. He gave me permission to think and to speak boldly about God.

During that time, I was finally becoming the Bible student that I always knew I should be. I truly developed a love for meditating and memorizing the Word of God. It was life-changing. I began to see the Bible as a description of God rather than a self-help book for me. As I scoured the pages, I began to understand and cherish the God of the Bible rather than the opinions of the culture. While training for ministry, I was given opportunities to preach and teach in different contexts. As often as I could, I would teach the attributes of God in some way. One of the first studies I ever did with a group of college students was the initial version of the outline of this book. I cherished each and every opportunity to teach others regarding the importance of knowing the biblically accurate attributes of God.

I drafted chapters of this book over the years, but fear of falling short kept putting it back on the shelf. Recently, I taught the attributes of God to a diverse group of men going through addiction recovery. As I walked men who were raised in the church and those who were having their first exposure in our presence, I once again realized the desperate nature of proper theology. We cannot love a God whom we do not know. We cannot follow God if we don't know his direction. After the completion of the study, I decided to number my days (Ps. 90:12) and get this book finished because I will never arrive at a place where I can adequately describe God in a manner of which he is worthy.

For some reason unknown to me, you have this copy in your hand right now. Due to a level of trust you have in me (which makes me tremble), a gift given to you on behalf of someone else (which makes me chuckle), or a random pickup by happenstance (which makes me anticipate), you have this content before you. My prayer is that God will use this book to flood your mind with biblical truth and overwhelm your soul with glorious wonder at the God who was and who is and who is to come. I hope that it will serve as a catalyst for you to engage in a lifelong pursuit of knowing the God of the Bible more.

To my family, thank you for allowing me the blessed opportunity of sharing what I'm still learning from the Bible as we sit around the table, curl up on the couch, adventure by the creek, or stretch out on your bedroom floor.

To my church family, thank you for pushing me to know God intimately and allowing me to speak of him boldly as we make a valiant effort of making disciples who make disciples.

To my God, "You have taught me from my youth, and I still proclaim your wondrous deeds" (Ps. 71:17). I have yet to get over you, and I suspect I never will.

CHAPTER 1
THE EDITABLE GOD

"Wiki" is a type of website that allows collaborative editing of its written content. You don't have to be an expert in computer coding or even the specific topic at hand before you are given complete expressive license to create and to edit the matter of such a site. The only expertise that is needed to contribute is the ability to think somewhat coherently and to express oneself through typed communication.

I believe we are living in a time that has taken this type of editable approach to theology. In this anti-authoritative, individualistic society, it is socially intolerant to be religiously intolerant. The culture teaches that what's good for you is good for you but not necessarily me. What I believe about my beliefs has absolutely no jurisdiction upon your own. The only unforgivable sin is holding to a worldview with such conviction that you feel inclined to share it with another. We are trained to allow someone to continue operating in perilous ignorance over warning them to any potential impending danger. In our society, we all believe something very antithetical from one another, and yet, somehow each of us is supposedly correct.

In lieu of divine revelation, we have sought out sideways collaboration. Instead of learning from the expert, we effortlessly become the expert. We have traded truths etched in stone by the finger of the Almighty God for erasable opinions jotted down on disposable coffeeshop napkins.

Our culture worships the Wiki God. We want ever so desperately to serve a deity whom we have the freedom and capability to edit. We cut out what we dislike about God. We copy a belief from another religion and paste it over into our own. This syncretistic approach places God upon a theological buffet in which we pick and choose those delicacies that we enjoy and pass over the dishes upon which we would rather not chew.

Voltaire said it this way: "In the beginning, God created man in his own image, and man has been trying to repay the favor ever since." I cannot disagree with him. We were made to be like God and not the other way around, yet we filter truth as soon as it conflicts with our preferences. When Scripture teaches an attribute of God that doesn't settle nicely into our neat, tidy theological cages that we have assembled, we resort to tossing out those doctrines altogether. "I just don't think God is like that" could be the theological slogan for our culture.

As gently as I can say this, please process this truth:

**It doesn't matter what you or I think about God.
It matters what God thinks about God.**

We must submit to the ultimate authority on such a significant matter and never frivolously choose to accept the societal flavor-of-the-month theology. If we plant our feet deep in our independent worldview stances, unwilling to change even when the truth is undeniably revealed, we will never reach a satisfying conclusion as individuals or as a culture. If we espouse beliefs based upon consensus, we will throw biblical doctrine overboard ever so eagerly and find ourselves unaware that we have entered far more dangerous waters. We will voyage at what seems to be a quicker, unhindered pace until we run ashore to our utter demise realizing far too late that the anchor that we thought was our captivity was instead our only salvation.

Truth does not hold us back. Truth keeps us up. If we pursue a biblical theology, we might be alarmed at how far off we are from God's characterizations of himself. The more we come to know about him, we may be shocked to realize how different he is from us. The psalmist declared God's position by stating, "You thought that I was one like yourself. But now I rebuke you and lay the charge before you" (Ps.

50:21). Have we been found guilty for assuming that God is positionally identifiable with us? Our opinions want to dictate that God should be qualitatively relatable, but we honestly do not want to experience the ramifications of living in a world governed by a God who was tailored by us. Our edited version of God would run this world into the ground because he would look too much like us.

ABSOLUTELY NO ABSOLUTES?

Nowadays, when one begins to use such dirty words such as "truth," the crowds begin to exclaim from the streets, "There is no absolute truth!" Well, is that statement absolutely true? "All truth is relative!" Apparently, all truths are relative except when it comes to that specific phrase. "That might be true for you but not for me." Can I say that about your statement? "You ought not to challenge someone else's beliefs" is, in reality, a challenge of someone's belief.

Postmodernism, also referred to as relativism, is the notion that there is no absolute truth. What's true for one does not mean it has to be necessarily true for another. Developed by the desire to see unity among humanity's search for truth, postmodernism has attempted to silence exclusivist religions from maintaining vital doctrinal stances. Those who hold this worldview believe that the only absolute truth allowed is when it pertains to their inclusive beliefs. Not only is this thinking religiously offensive but it is rationally absurd.

No matter how hard we try to put the theological backspace within everyone's reach, we must quickly acknowledge the frivolous nature of such an attempt. Allowing everyone to come up with their unique version of God does not help us come closer to understanding God. What appears as valiant efforts to know God are actually devious attempts to dethrone God. Unadulterated truth must be pursued and never neglected for something inherently lesser.

Oftentimes, in the quest for such a noble purpose, we substitute God's eternal truth for our temporal opinion. We can see the goal up ahead in the distance, but it honestly isn't the destination at which we thought we would arrive. Jaded by scratching the surface of such a startling discovery, we would rather elect a new leader and draft a new constitution. In our pride, we believe that if we can just recast the lead part, then we can rewrite the script and create a more satisfactory final presentation.

In the Bible, the devil is depicted as a fallen angel (2 Pet. 2:4) who tried that exact thing. Consumed by pride (Ezek. 28:17), he wanted to take God's throne for himself (Isa. 14:13). He is known for having the audacity of questioning and even challenging God's methods (Job 1:9-11; 2:4-5). When he tempted the first couple of the Bible, he deceived them by playing to a desire shared with him – to know what God knows (Gen. 3:5). If they know what God knows, they don't have to rely on him anymore for this coveted knowledge. More than merely the apprehension of information, they wanted to craft the very definition of knowledge. They wanted the authority to discern what was right and what was wrong. If they could obtain this power, they would pridefully wield the ability to take God's place. They can redraft the sacred textbook and procure a desired state of fluid theology.

Adam and Eve chose to believe a lie over the truth. The falsity was more palatable. The devil's deceit was indeed more convenient. This couple preferred a deity of their own making versus the Maker himself. They tried to rewrite what he said and fundamentally remake who he is. They wanted to replace God.

This line of thinking did not dissipate with Eden's eviction. The desire to make God play by our ever-changing rules still lures us today. We throw out the truth and replace it with our opinions. Our culture is currently experiencing moral anarchy because we have attempted to remove the possibility of divine authority.

Our subconscious reveals our double-standards concerning doctrine. We don't want to be told what to believe, by God or anyone else, but we think that our beliefs should be eagerly accepted and celebrated by all. How can we coexist in a world when our opinions concerning God are so vast in scope?

The campaign to coexist religiously urges people to avoid any sense of staunch doctrinal loyalty. The problem is that many religions do call for unwavering allegiance. While I am the first to admit that many of history's darkest moments came under the influence of those thinking they were doing God's work, we cannot throw out religious devotion due to some extremists' religious distortion.

Truth can never be determined by a vote or a committee. The essence of truth makes its very nature absolute. Truth must also be timeless and universal. Any doctrine worth believing must be able to be regarded as true by any person in any location at any time, or else it is simply not the truth. If one belief is acceptable for you but not for me, it is a blatant falsehood. One or both of us is undoubtedly incorrect.

If I think God is pleased with our society and you think he is disgusted, can we both be correct? If I am a staunch believer that God intervenes throughout history and you believe that he is the ancient watchmaker who set the cogs and wheels in motion but then turned it loose to let it be, can we be talking about the same God? If I think God empathizes with my greatest sorrow and you think he is too lofty to depress himself with whiners like me, don't you see that at least one of us is terribly, terribly wrong?

This conflict complicates our discovery for the answer to the question concerning the character of God. It reveals the fact that if we rely on each other's opinions concerning the divine, we only possess mere personal sentiments with which to disagree. Opinions devoid of any apparent authority will continue to enable religious conflicts that have plagued history.

A.W. Tozer was a lofty theologian and passionate pastor of the twentieth century. In his book, *The Knowledge of the Holy*, he presented a thesis statement that signifies the importance of addressing this issue. He wrote:

"What comes to your mind when you think about God is the most important thing about you."

On the first read, that statement may seem a bit dramatic, but is he on to something here? If someone thinks that God is a lighting-bolt throwing angry titan in the sky, that person will carefully calculate how he or she lives his or her life. If someone thinks God could care less about the chaotic condition of this planet, that person will probably not seek God for help amidst growing concerns. If someone assumes that God does not exist, the only accountability that a person can have is himself or herself.

What comes to your mind when you think about God might be the most important thing about you. If Tozer is correct with the thought that our theological beliefs have the power to change every element of our lives, it is of utmost importance to make sure that our convictions are painstakingly accurate. If what comes to my mind when I think about God is the most important thing about me, then I better ensure that what comes to my mind when I think about God is actually correct.

I desperately need truth. If truth does exist, it is far superior and more enduring than my flighty opinions. What God says about God is far more dependable than what I say about God.

"WHO DO YOU SAY I AM?"

One of the stories that repeatedly has come to my mind even as I type these words is an encounter Jesus had with Peter one day. Jesus once asked Peter's opinion concerning his own identity. At the time when Jesus asked this question to Peter, the ministry of Jesus was booming. Everywhere he went, people followed him just to see what he would do or what he would say next.

Peter had a front-row seat to it all. He remembered what it was like when Jesus turned one boy's lunch into a satisfying feast for thousands. Not only could he remember the taste of that meal but he knew what it was like to haul the leftovers all the way home (Matt. 14:20). Peter experienced the joy and gratitude from his entire family when Jesus healed his mother-in-law from sickness. He watched with amazement as this woman who was uncharacteristically sidelined by fever and unable to enjoy her company was immediately serving the people in her home due to a single touch from Jesus (Matt. 8:14-15).

Peter saw Jesus cause the blind to see, the mute to speak, the deaf to hear, the lame to walk, the demons to flee, and even the dead to rise.

The region was abuzz. Everyone had an opinion concerning Jesus. In one of those earth-shattering conversations prompted by Jesus, he asked his disciples concerning the public consensus regarding his own identity. The disciples began to relay information of which he was already aware. He just listened intently.

They reported, "Some say John the Baptist, others say Elijah, and others Jeremiah or one of the prophets" (Matt. 16:14).

After giving them his full attention, he then asked a simple question that would forever change history. He said to them, "But who do you say that I am?"

Simon Peter replied, "You are the Christ, the Son of the living God."

Jesus answered him, "Blessed are you, Simon Bar-Jonah! For flesh and blood has not revealed this to you, but my Father who is in heaven. And I tell you, you are Peter, and on this rock, I will build my church, and the gates of hell shall not prevail against it" (Matt. 16:15-18).

I was taught this account by many who emphasized that at this moment it didn't matter who Jesus was; it mattered who Jesus was to Peter. Jesus' objective truth was useless if it wasn't a subjective reality. That line of thinking is simply an unbiblical lie originating in the pit of hell. Peter didn't ace Jesus' pop quiz because his answer was personal; he aced it because he was correct.

If Peter would have said, "I have to agree with the crowds. I think you are simply another prophet," Jesus would not have congratulated him. "Jesus, there have been a lot of talented preachers before you, and there will be many after you who can do precisely what you are doing. Don't get me wrong – you are a great guy, but that's just it – you are just a great guy and not a great God."

With an answer like that, Jesus would not have responded in such a positive manner. He would not have praised Peter for his individualistic theory if his conclusion was incorrect. Jesus would never have built his church on a simple fisherman's flattering hypothesis. More than sentiment, Jesus was after truth.

If you study the life and teachings of Christ, you can guarantee that he would not have responded, "You know, Peter, that's not exactly what I was hoping you would say, but who am I to make such an exclusive claim to truth? If it's true to you, then I think that's just great. How could I argue with such a sincere display of authentic honesty? Let's all gather around to sing 'Kumbaya' and have a big, tolerant group hug."

Jesus was never known to behave that way. Regarding truth, Jesus is gracious but not tolerant. He is too loving to allow error to continue without intervention.

Jesus built his church on the truth – not on the opinion.

Peter grasped the fact that Jesus was the long-awaited Messiah. Jesus was the one whom the people of God had been longing to behold. Everything in the Old Testament had connected the dots and colored in the picture of who this Messiah would be, and standing before Peter was the brilliantly vivid Jesus the Christ – the actual son of the living God. The King had come, and the Kingdom was coming! This encounter is one of the few times in the gospels that Peter nailed something without a hint of error.

Jesus responded with a play on words that you may or may not have caught at first glance. "Bar-Jonah" means son of Jonah. Jesus praised Peter for his answer and essentially said, "Simon, your earthly father didn't reveal that to you, but your Heavenly Father did. I am going to change your name to reflect that you are a part of a different family now. Welcome to the family of God."

How did Simon Peter get it right? Because it was accurately revealed to him by none other than God. Man doesn't discover the truth; God reveals the truth. Jesus promised to build the Church upon the stalwart rock of Peter's confession. At that moment, Peter understood that Jesus is the ultimate fulfillment of truth. Peter knew it, he confessed it, and Christ vowed that his followers would build the Church not on man's opinion but upon God's truth.

WHEN JESUS CALLS YOU SATAN

For all the fumbling mistakes for which Peter is remembered, here is a glorious example of a moment when he was undeniably correct, and history would ultimately never be the same again. Riding on such a momentous spiritual occasion, Peter should have known the importance of exiting on a high note, but unfortunately, he opened his mouth moments later to reveal how quickly we can fall from such theological prominence. In light of Peter's confession, Jesus began to unveil some previously concealed information. His path was clearly leading him to Jerusalem, and he was confident that he would soon suffer unjustly under the hands of the authorities who would brutally murder him there. Since the disciples were now cognizant of his identity, he wanted to prepare them for what was coming his way, and he wanted them to know he would not change course just because suffering was imminent.

Still beaming from the honorary theological doctorate he had just received from none other than Jesus the Christ, Peter decided to pull the Messiah over to the side for a little constructively critical chitchat. Apparently, Jesus was confused, and Peter's glowing spiritual intellect was required to clear things up. Peter took him aside and began to rebuke him, saying, "Far be it from you, Lord! This shall never happen to you."

But he turned and said to Peter, "Get behind me, Satan! You are a hindrance to me. For you are not setting your mind on the things of God, but on the things of man" (Matt. 16:22-23).

Jesus' suffering didn't fit well into Peter's Christological framework. This type of path is not what Peter envisioned. The cross would distort the image of whom Peter thought the Christ should be. Jesus was revealing the truth to Peter, and Peter didn't resonate with the content and, therefore, desired to change it.

God made Peter in his image, and now Peter wanted to repay the favor. He envisioned following a God who knew no suffering. The picture of the Messiah present in Peter's mind was that of the victor and not the victim. Peter didn't like whom God was turning out to be, and so he attempted to change him.

Moments after Jesus renamed Simon as Peter, he suddenly nicknamed him Satan. Should it be to our surprise that Jesus called Peter by the name of the first one who tried to modify the identity of God? Satan endeavored to alter the personality and the activity of God, and Peter was following in his sacrilegious footsteps. Don't miss Jesus' diagnosis: Peter was not thinking about God; he was thinking about Man (Matt. 16:23). He wanted God to be more like him.

So do we. When we begin to discover that God is not like whom we thought he should be, we desperately want him to adjust to a mirroring type of expectations. Even if our thought processes stem from a desire to assist God in the public relations department, those efforts are in vain. Jesus interprets such blatant endeavors as mutiny. Venturing to improve God is downright satanic, and he will vehemently oppose any such efforts.

If you're going to stay clear of Jesus calling you devilish monikers, then avoid any attempts at altering his identity. Stop trying to change God and learn to embrace God. No matter how hard we try to revere the Wiki God, this deity is virtually impossible to grasp. The characteristics have changed yet again by the time we finish reading the last draft. If we attempt to recreate the Uncreated One in our image, we will find ourselves worshipping ourselves before too long.

THE ATTRIBUTES OF GOD

In the following pages, I want to address some misguided thinking. While worldly theology is present in our culture, weak theology is often present within our churches. Instead of editing who God is to suit my fancy or your expectations, I am going to apply to a higher authority than even you and me. I am going to utilize Scripture to help illuminate us concerning what God thinks about himself.

In each chapter, I will begin by presenting a common misconception of who God is. Specific recurring themes seem to invade our theologies. After describing these dangerous wiki submissions, I pray that through scriptural teaching, God will help to countermeasure our misunderstandings. We will arrive at what theologians call the biblical attributes of God. The attributes are specific characteristics taught in the Bible that help us understand the character and conduct of God. As we look at themes throughout Scripture that traces his heart and his hand, we will experience a fuller understanding of who he is.

At the end of this offering, you hopefully won't be taking my word for it. My remarks are by far the most dispensable content within these pages. I want to present you with what the Bible teaches concerning theology, and you will have to wrestle with its claims. I have. There are specific attributes that are hard for me to accept because I have found out that God is not like me. He is utterly other than me. Within the whole counsel of God (Acts 20:27), we find that God the Father, God the Son, and God the Spirit are worshiped and revered. While God is reliable, he is rarely predictable. He doesn't always operate the way we think he should. At every stage within the redemptive narrative, God's reveals his character more fully. With each stroke of inspired revelation, we behold a more glorious and somewhat surprising picture of who he really is.

In many theological studies, scholars will divide God's attributes into a list of those which are communicable and incommunicable. Communicable attributes are those which he "shares" with humanity. God is love. We also have the capacity to love, so, therefore, the attribute of love is communicable.

Incommunicable attributes are those that only God can possess. God is omniscient which means he knows absolutely everything. Since we do not know everything, this attribute of omniscience is incommunicable.

Due to God's otherness, I have to disagree with this commonly held distinction between the two categories. God's all-knowing ability compared to my scope of limited knowledge is just as vast in differentiation as is his commitment to unwavering, unconditional love as compared to my expressions of frivolous, conditional love. Compared to God, all of his attributes are incommunicable when positioned side by side with the quality of one like me.

God is entirely set apart from me. He is not only holy, but he is holy, holy, holy. To accept God as-is as portrayed in Scripture is a challenge to my head but a delight to my soul.

When God's descriptions of God's character within God's Word confronts our claims to individualistic theorizations, we are each forced to respond. What will we do with this claim to truth? Will we accept God's Word or attempt to make it fit our agenda? I had to choose and so will you. You will decide to follow God the Maker or the god you make. Each of us will elect to marvel at the Grand Designer or esteem our grand design. I implore you to engage yourself with the biblical text concerning the attributes of God and allow its truth to remedy what theological infections are possibly poisoning your soul.

I don't want your version of God. You don't need my version of God. We just desperately need God.

✂ **ATTRIBUTES** REVIEW

Incorrect Perception: ~~God is editable~~.

Correct Belief: *God is God without our permission.*

Focal Verse: *These things you have done, and I have been silent; you thought that I was one like yourself. But now I rebuke you and lay the charge before you (Ps. 50:21).*

Implication: *God's version of himself is superior to your version of him.*

🗐 **FURTHER** STUDY

What specific thought from this chapter challenged you?

Meditate on Psalm 115. Write out any phrases from this psalm that get your attention.

"Our God is in the heavens; he does all that he pleases" (Ps. 115:3). List some specific rights that God has.

CORRECTIVE THEOLOGY

Why is it irrational to believe that God should allow all people to think whatever they want to about him?

Is there an area about God in which you honestly desire to change? What is it?

Why is God's version of himself always superior to our versions?

CHAPTER 2
THE NEEDY GOD

Many people express allegiance to the Needy God. In all honesty, they show obeisance to him because they are worried about what will happen to him if they fail to oblige. Without mankind's existence, God's presence seemingly lacks a clear purpose. It is difficult to envision what he even did before we arrived on the scene. In fact, the reality of our existence centers around addressing God's supposed neediness. God was apparently lonely, but ever since he created us, we have graciously alleviated his solitudinous sorrow.

I first learned about the Needy God from well-intended spiritual mentors. In an effort to draw me near to God, they depicted him as destitute. They explained the reason why loved ones died is that God must have needed them in heaven for some definitive reason. Many of these leaders would teach me that God wanted to do certain things in my life but was unable because I was unwilling. They explained that if I really expected God to do something in this world, he needs my money, resources, and volunteer hours to get the job done. With so many responsibilities, he must be relieved that he created me to help him out.

It even seemed as if God's emotional state was contingent upon my regular availability for him. At an early age, I was taught regularly concerning the necessity of having a daily quiet time in which I would commit to reading my Bible and praying to him. To ensure that I didn't cancel that appointment, I was taught that God's emotional wholeness and my daily obedience were intrinsically linked. "How do you think God feels when none of his children even want to spend time with him? If you don't read your Bible and pray in the morning, God is left abandoned in heaven wondering why you don't care anything about him. After all he has done for you, how do you think that makes him feel?"

Guilt is a reasonably potent motivator for me. When I envisioned God as a senile, old man stranded in the nursing home with no recent visitors, I felt a legitimate burden to spend time with him. If I neglected that time, he might become depressed or lonely, and how then would the world continue to orbit within the cosmos? If God is that needy, the state of the world is instead dependent upon us. I was exhorted at an early age that I better never let God down. The only way I can let God down is if I was holding him up in the first place.

God is not needy. God is independent.

THE INDEPENDENCE OF GOD

The attribute of God's independence is of extreme importance. Sometimes this attribute is described as God's self-existence. Others will use the term, "aseity," which means one's existence can only originate from oneself. Nothing outside of the being can take the credit for that ultimate existence.

The concept is simple to communicate but challenging to grasp: God is without origin. He is the uncreated Creator. He is the causeless cause. Nothing existed before God, and God needs absolutely nothing to exist in order to prove his divine nature. The Creator does not require anything from the creation. In order to be God, he must be unequivocally absent of need. For if he needs something, that reveals him to be incomplete. God cannot be deficient.

As the Apostle Paul visited Athens, he encountered the numerous statues venerating the plentiful gods. As he stared down men who were worshiping the objects of their own making, he felt compelled to confront their error. "The God who made the world and everything in it, being Lord of heaven and earth, does not live in temples made by man, nor is he served by human hands, *as though he needed anything*, since he himself gives to all mankind life and breath and everything" (Acts 17:24-25). Paul showed the hopelessness of any man's religious devotion if given to a deity created by man. Anyone who has to make his or her own god (Ps. 115:4) will become like that god one day (Ps. 115:8).

Paul did not follow the Needy God. He scoffed at the notion. When Paul commented, "as though he needed anything" (Acts 17:25), he was elevating the people's perception of the one true God. He revealed the pitiful nature of having to fabricate anything for a deity. If a god requires a man to form him, that god's resiliency must be severely compromised. The ability to identify as God assumes complete and utter independence.

We cannot create anything for the Creator. Paul believed in the one who needed no creation. This God defined himself. Paul's belief in God's independence originated from scriptural teaching. Inspired by God, these teachings were recorded by the likes of Job, Moses, Asaph, Isaiah, and others. Paul knew the Old Testament and knew it well. So, let's start at the beginning of that book and at the beginning of this world.

"In the beginning, God created the heavens and the earth" (Gen. 1:1). Even the phrase, "in the beginning, God created," is fundamentally an implication that God existed even before there was a beginning! Before everything began, God already was. He was not dependent upon any other thing to live. God utilized no pre-existing matter to exist. God *is* the pre-existing matter. His steps even precede when there was a world to walk upon. He actually set the planet on its very foundation (Ps. 104:5). No person was even around to help him when he settled the globe's infrastructure (Job 38:4). Even the very heavens are the work of his hands (Ps. 102:25).

This God created every single thing in the universe (Rev. 4:11). All the diversified elements of creation find only one commonality - their Creator. In his wisdom, he was able to make all of the universe's manifold works (Ps. 104:24). The only way to create all things is if you are before all things. The Apostle John taught that not only were all things invoked by the Godhead, but he made sure to emphasize that nothing has been made that was not caused by him (John 1:3). The belief in one God assumes that he is the one from who are all things and for whom we all exist (1 Cor. 8:6). "For from him and through him and to him are all things. To him be glory forever. Amen" (Rom. 11:36).

All things were created *by* him and *for* him (Col. 1:16). He is not only the originator but the purpose as well. His existence before all things provides the essence of the stability needed for all things to hold together in him (Col. 1:17). He is known as the Ancient of Days (Dan. 7:9, 13, 22). He is God from everlasting to everlasting (Ps. 90:2). As the eternal God (Gen. 21:33), he precedes every single other element in the universe. He has no end to his years (Ps. 102:27). He is the first, and he is the last (Isa. 44:6; 48:12). He is the Alpha and the Omega who lives forevermore (Rev. 1:17-18).

God has life *in* himself (John 5:26). God's being does not originate outside of himself because it was not given to him by another. No external source provided him life or purpose for nothing outside him could ever hope to add value to him. He established every ounce of his being from within his own person.

Faith itself is dependent upon the fundamental belief in God's independence. "And without faith, it is impossible to please him, for whoever would draw near to God must believe that he exists and that he rewards those who seek him" (Heb. 11:6). A Christian's faith begins with a belief in God's existence. For God to be God, his identity demands the attribute of independence. He is the ultimate subsistence. There has never been a moment when God was not, and there will never be a moment when God will not be.

When God approached Moses from within the burning bush, he called on this shepherd to lead the Israelites out of slavery. Moses would have to confront the Egyptian Pharaoh who governed as if he was a god and who also venerated countless other gods. Before Moses could accept the assignment, he at least needed the ability to namedrop some deity into the impending conversation. Pharaoh would refuse to continue such a pointless discussion if he was unsure which of the many gods Moses was citing to free the Israelites. What name should

Moses use to describe this particular God to such a pagan ruler in such a pantheonic land?

"God said to Moses, 'I AM WHO I AM'" (Exod. 3:14). With other gods, a designator was required for identification. Ra was the god of the sun, Mafdet was the god of justice, and Thoth was the god of wisdom. The gods were known by a certain percentage of appropriately-assigned deified duties. Yet, when the God of the Bible chose a name, he simply stated, "I AM WHO I AM." He is who he is. He will be who he says he will be. God is the independent, self-existent one who defines himself. To utilize a designator for this God would be futile because his existence is not dependent upon any of his works. He is God by the very proof of his own existence.

THE AWARENESS WE NEED

When studying God's attributes, one must ask the question, "In light of this truth, how now should I think. What am I to do?" When our humanity intersects with his divinity, what damage is left from the unavoidable collision? In the case of God's independence, this truth needs no one to impact. In fact, none of God's attributes actually need human subjects on which to establish themselves. The sun does not need sunburned skin to prove its intensity, and neither does God need our scorched souls to prove his worth.

And yet therein lies the complexity of it all. We have seen the light. We have experienced the warmth. God possesses no responsibility to expose us to his glory and yet he does. "What is man that you are mindful of him, and the son of man that you care for him" (Ps. 8:4)? This truth should serve to give us the self-awareness that is essential for our often misguided souls. We can't provide anything that God needs because he is entirely without need. We are impotent negotiators with him. We cannot barter with him because we have nothing of intrinsic worth to place upon the table.

When confronting the innocent sufferer Job, God asked, "Who has first given to me, that I should repay him? Whatever is under the whole heaven is mine" (Job 41:11). If God were needy and required something as simple as a meal, he wouldn't even ask us because all the world and its fullness belong to him (Ps. 50:12). Where would we even begin to haggle with him?

God's independence should create in us significant insignificance. God is entirely absent of need, and we are entirely devoid of any necessary caliber. God doesn't need us. Never once has God required our involvement to address one of his problems. God has never been stressed out by any situation. He has never frantically paced the halls of heaven gathering an angelic poll on what to do or how to do it. The Lord of hosts has never once attempted to recruit and remained anxious about the results. God may appreciate our efforts, but he has never once relied upon our efforts. Instead of allowing that truth to discourage you, it should solidify you.

God doesn't need you, but he wants you.

Take Esther for example. She was a fair damsel who caught the eye of a pagan king. He had just rid himself of his previous obstinate wife (Esth. 2:1) and was holding a beauty contest to determine his next lucky yet endangered partner (Esth. 2:2). As an exiled Jewish woman living in an idolatrous land, she had to play it safe regarding her people and her religion. Even as Esther became his queen, she was acutely aware of the possible peril if she upset the dynamics in her new family and how it could impact her kinsmen who were spread throughout the kingdom.

She played it safe until her Uncle Mordecai made known to her a plot to kill all the Jewish people (Esth. 4:1). Many people recount his speech and explain that Esther came to the kingdom for "such a time as this." Since she had this position and had the power to stop this massacre, she seemed to be the savior of the people. It was evident that her placement was providential. If it weren't for Esther, what would the people have done?

If you look at the entire phrase, you see exactly what the people would have done. Nothing. They would have done absolutely zilch. They would have anticipated the Independent God to do what only he could do. How could they envision putting their trust in a mere person? Mordecai spells it out clearly. "For if you keep silent at this time, relief and deliverance will rise from the Jews from *another place*, but you and your father's house will perish. And *who knows* whether you have not come to the kingdom for such a time as this?" (Esth. 4:14).

Did you catch it? Esther wasn't the savior. God wasn't dependent upon her. If she failed to play her role, someone else would step in and take over. Relief and deliverance would come from the Jews from any other potential candidate that God saw fit. Why? Because God planned to keep the Jews alive, and no person was critical enough to jeopardize his foreordained outcome. He was going to bless all the nations of the world through this people (Gen. 12:3; Isa. 49:6), and God's purposes could not and would not be thwarted (Isa. 14:27; Job 42:2). The Israelites had no danger of perishing due to the promised one who was coming. God's plan would go forward with or without Esther. Her position near a temporal throne had been installed by the one on the eternal throne. He was not short on options if she failed to do what she had been called to do.

God didn't need Esther, but he wanted Esther. In all honesty, I think there is more beauty in that truth than in the alternative. If God needed me or anyone else, he immediately ceases to be God and fear would instantaneously arrest my soul. But to grasp that God is not dependent upon any of us yet chooses to use us is a humbling truth of which I pray I never grow weary of rehearsing in my mind. God doesn't need me, but he wants me. God isn't dependent upon me, but he is invested in me. God isn't lacking, yet he is still inviting. He doesn't need my skills for the task at hand, but he would like me to follow him to work anyway.

God is not needy. He is not dependent. The universe will continue the previously planned operational schedule with or without any of us. We can join him on the frontlines or watch him from the nosebleeds. He isn't anxious as he awaits our willingness to be involved. And yet, we are invited. Oh, what glorious wonder! God's invitation never comes out of desperation. He is independent, yet he wants to include us. The fact that God is devoid of need and yet includes us anyway should cause us to stand in awe.

✂ INDEPENDENCE REVIEW

Incorrect Perception: ~~God is needy~~.

Correct Attribute: *God is independent.*

Definition: *The independence of God means that he is entirely without need.*

Focal Verse: *Nor is he served by human hands, as though he needed anything, since he himself gives to all mankind life and breath and everything (Acts 17:25).*

Implication: *God doesn't need you, but he wants you.*

🗎 FURTHER STUDY

What specific thought from this chapter encouraged you to think differently?

Meditate on Psalm 50:7-15. Write out any phrases from this passage that get your attention.

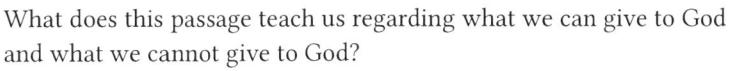

What does this passage teach us regarding what we can give to God and what we cannot give to God?

How does God's independence challenge popular beliefs within religious circles?

How does this attribute challenge your personal theology?

If you were truly to believe in God's independence, how would it specifically change you today?

CHAPTER 3
THE MAN UPSTAIRS GOD

Many people casually refer to God as the man upstairs. Minimizing the unthinkable chasm between his quality and our quality, they diminish his character as someone only slightly higher than us. This diluted theology merely ascribes the teensiest superiority to God. In this line of thinking, his being is impressive but not actually overwhelming. God made us in his image. We did not make God in our image. People wrongly assume that God's magnitude is just marginally higher than ours. By elevating our stance upon our tippy toes, we think that we can peer eyeball to eyeball with the man upstairs in order to make him our relatable peer. We readily accept that he is more prominent than us but just by mere degree.

As we, tragically mistaken theologians, gauge beings on a man-made scale, we will give God the clear advantage but seek to limit his apparent prestige. In this type of elementary thinking, plants aren't as great as animals, animals aren't as great as people, people aren't as great as angels, and angels aren't as great as God. While the increasing value of worth does modify at some points as you progress through this list of beings, it is not incremental at every level. God is more than merely a superior human with a little more knowledge and power. For if God could be incrementally greater than each level of being, that would imply that the gulf between would be potentially bridgeable. If you do not perceive him to be supremely higher in the same way over all different things, then your perspective of him is not high enough. He is more than marginally superior to us.

God is not the man upstairs. God is transcendent.

THE TRANSCENDENCE OF GOD

To appreciate the glorious grandeur of God, we must step back and see him for who he truly is. Surprisingly, he's a lot bigger than you ever imagined. He is genuinely higher than you thought possible. His magnificence will utterly surprise you. God transcends even our expectations.

The transcendence of God means that he greatly surpasses our human worth and experience. Something transcendent exceeds far beyond our limitations. With this understanding, God is the only absolutely transcendent being. He is far beyond our capacity. Since God is the only uncreated one, every other being is created and therefore, somewhat approachable and manageable.

The natural line of thinking regarding God's transcendence is to picture him as higher than us. While that thought is accurate, this particular attribute is not about him being impressively taller or having a prestigious skyline view from the top floor. His transcendence is all about his unthinkable and unattainable worth that far surpasses anything we could ever possibly imagine.

Our pitiful verbiage is littered with our unsuspecting attempts to belittle him. Whether it is referring to God as the man upstairs or Jesus as our homeboy, we futilely attempt to shrink him down to our piteous size. Why should we be surprised that we possess such small faith when we even minify his existence so much within our church gatherings?

Our worship has grown lifeless, dull, and, frankly, unfitting. We lead people in worship without developing within them a longing for the object of our worship. Our lackluster attempts to encounter him reveal that we are unaware of the profound privilege that he desires to meet with us at all. The fire of our communion with him has been frostbitten by our complacency. Listen to certain songs we sing and be lulled to a sickening slumber and a doxological drudgery. Some of our lyrics are so pathetic because their depictions lack an aura of grandeur. Their lines are so vague and elementary that it causes us to look down on God rather than to look up to him. If we can replace the name of "God" with "baby" in some lyrics and it would make them instantaneously suffice as a juvenile love song, we have a severe worship problem.

Our prayers have also been neutered. While I am all for approaching God as Father, sometimes we forget that he is still our "Father in heaven." I cringe when someone's voice and vocabulary lack a level of respect that God deserves. Yes, he is our Heavenly Father, but if your earthly father wouldn't have accepted such disrespectful levity in your speech towards him, why are we satisfied to offer one higher even less? When we pray, does it seem like we are talking to the one who is so mesmerizingly beyond us and yet so amazingly beside us?

Even our sermons have lost the fire of wonder regarding who we are speaking about. If a sermon sounds more about us than it does about God, we are tragically focusing on a lesser topic and should assume feeble results. A self-help motivational speech does not belong in the sanctuaries of the redeemed! If we could help ourselves, we don't need God. Before a preacher tell us what we ought to do, we must be aware of the seismic power of whom he speaks. How tragically often can people leave a sermon and fail to be awestricken by the blinding magnitude of the Almighty God!

When we fail to speak, sing, pray, and preach of God in such a way that causes our souls to ache for the needed awe of the immense presence of the Almighty God, we do those around us a devilish disservice. If he is diminished in the church, he is definitely disregarded in the culture. If God's people are unable to handle him fittingly, what hope do others have? God is God – there is none higher than he! There is none so great as God! I beg us to wake up and realize the unthinkable infinitude of this glorious God that we claim to follow. If we were truly to grasp how transcendent he is, it would change our peculiar, pitiful perceptions.

So, exactly how is God transcendent? First, God transcends our worth. He is most high over all the earth and exalted leagues above every god of our making (Ps. 97:9). God's value is so superior to ours, we can't even begin to search through his greatness because we would get lost in it (Ps. 145:3). When was the last time that you became overwhelmed by the grandeur and power and glory and victory and majesty that belongs to the only God (1 Chr. 29:11)? When the prophet Isaiah saw the Lord, he saw him high and lifted up (Isa. 6:1). When God is depicted in the Scriptures, he is surrounded by angelic beings incessantly proclaiming his greatness (Isa. 6:2-3; Rev. 4:8). How their vantage point could remedy us of our mediocre perspectives infecting our theology and doxology!

Second, God transcends our understanding. We are unable even to comprehend his actions. His thoughts and ways are so much higher than ours, Isaiah said that they equaled the difference between the earth and the heavens (Isa. 55:8-9). His all-encompassing understanding positions us unable to hide from his glorious presence (Jer. 23:24; Ps. 139:7). While our inability to understand certain situations fully can frustrate us, our intermediate understanding of God's transcendent knowledge should cause us to revel in who he is and not be dependent upon who we can become.

Third, God transcends our capacity. We are limited, yet God knows no limit. How could we even dare assume that we could discover all the deep things of God and research the boundaries of the Almighty if he is even higher than heaven itself (Job 11:7-10)? How foolish do we attempt to design buildings to honor him when even the highest heaven cannot contain him (1 Kgs. 8:27). The truly immortal one dwells in unapproachable light upon which we cannot dare to gaze (1 Tim. 6:16). He is the great God and the great King above all gods whose hand simultaneously dwell in the depths of the earth and the heights of the mountains (Ps. 95:3-5).

Fourth, God transcends our capability. He is competent and capable to do everything outside of our scopes. God stretched out the north and hung the world on absolutely nothing (Job 26:7). When even the pillars of heaven tremble at his rebuke (Job 26:11), how overwhelming it is to entertain what his unfiltered presence would do to us? And yet these mighty works of which he allows us to comprehend in some finite fashion are described as the mere fringes of his ways (Job 26:14).

He sits high above the world, and humanity's grandest representatives appear like grasshoppers to him (Isa. 40:22).

Finally, God transcends our rationale. He has never once been mandated to act in a way that fits our expectations. When he breaks in, there is no way for us to subdue or alter his moving. We expect him to come when we call and to perform as we desire, but his presence is not summoned or is his timing dictated by mere needy individuals like ourselves. Initially experiencing God is not necessarily a comfortably natural encounter when depicted within the Scriptures. Abraham repented in dust and ashes (Gen. 18:27), Jacob was mesmerized by God's presence (Gen. 28:17), Job covered his mouth (Job 40:4), Isaiah tried to hide (Isa. 6:5), Daniel fell down as if he was dead (Dan. 10:15-17), and Peter begged Jesus to leave his presence when arrested by his shame (Luke 5:8). If you truly understand who you are encountering, you will never be the same again. Just like Jacob wrestling with God brought about a lifetime of staggering due to a dislocated hip (Gen. 32:31), we cannot walk away the same after bumping into God. The people who have genuinely encountered God never walk with a swagger but only a limp.

THE PERSPECTIVE WE NEED

If God is so much higher than us, what does that mean about us? Does this truth make you feel small? No matter how terribly demeaning that might seem to you at first, that decreased perspective is a very welcomed thing for your soul. In fact, you need to realize you aren't as high as you once supposed yourself to be.

When you begin to experience a mere fraction of the splendor of God while understanding your insignificant nature compared to him, shouldn't that reveal the colossal distance? Quite the opposite. Attempting to acknowledge the vast difference between you two should cause you to realize this life-changing truth: the God high above has come far down below due to his love for you.

David summarizes it beautifully: "For though the LORD is high, he regards the lowly, but the haughty he knows from afar" (Ps. 138:6).

Isaiah records it this way: "For thus says the One who is high and lifted up, who inhabits eternity, whose name is Holy: 'I dwell in the high and holy place, and also with him who is of a contrite and lowly spirit, to revive the spirit of the lowly, and to revive the heart of the contrite'" (Isa. 57:15). A God so high, so immense, so transcendent should discard such trivial creatures like us, and yet he becomes one of us (John 1:14; Phil. 2:7) to bring us closer to himself.

As a child, I found such amusement in a sketch that Grover regularly performed on Sesame Street. "Near. Far." He repeatedly called out as he ran forwards and backward from the camera. As he ran closer to the camera and shouted, "near," his appearance seemed to grow magically larger. As he retreated to the back of the room and yelled out, "far," his image gradually seemed microscopic. When Grover moved back and forth, did his size change? Of course not, but my perception of him did.

It's the same way regarding the transcendence of God. Why does God seem high and lifted up at some times and low and disregarded at other times? It is definitely not his fault. God doesn't grow more prominent, but my perception of him does.

In fact, the closer that I get to him, the more transcendent I discover him to be. The deeper I plunge into the Word, the further I push into prayer, and the more frequent I catch him on the move, the more significant I perceive him to be. The closer I get to him, the further I have to look up. God looked massive from afar, but the closer I get, the more imposing he appears to be, and the lesser I acknowledge myself to be. Like Job, I can't help but exclaim, "I had heard of you by the hearing of the ear, but now my eye sees you; therefore I despise myself, and repent in dust and ashes" (Job 42:5-6).

Isaiah saw God as transcendent at a pivotal time in his life. He described it as a time that when his earthly king was down in death's grasp (Isa. 6:1), he saw his heavenly King (Isa. 6:5) as high and lifted up upon life's throne (Isa. 6:1). Angelic beings called seraphim served in the presence of the LORD and are so stupendously stellar that they have six wings. As someone who doesn't even possess one wing, I can't even comprehend what one would do with six without Isaiah describing it for us. These compelling beings took two of them to cover their faces due to the sheer blinding light from the magnificent brilliance of God (Isa. 6:2).

God's presence was so transcendent at that moment that the entire temple was filled up with the mere train of his robe. Foundations were shaking, the house was smoking, and Isaiah was trembling. God wasn't growing in reality, but he was in Isaiah's perspective. The prophet had the only appropriate response. He didn't try to approach God as his peer. He didn't run away in fear. He made a simple admission: "Woe is me! For I am lost; for I am a man of unclean lips, and I dwell in the midst of a people of unclean lips; for my eyes have seen the King, the LORD of hosts!" (Isa. 6:5).

In the presence of God, Isaiah was more fixated on God's glory than his own worth. Being arrested by the splendor of God never made Isaiah feel better about himself. He rejoiced in God and despaired in himself. In fact, God's grand transcendence provided the needed humility in the prophet's life before his ministry began.

Isaiah saw God for how infinitely transcendent he really was, and he never fully recovered from it. Have we? In our negligent lunacy, have we attempted to regulate the movement of God by venturing to tame him? Are we trying to retract him till he is on our approved peer level? This God is too glorious to be domesticated into some safe version. He is so far beyond even our ability to reform him into some desired adaptation.

The worse thing I could do for my soul would be attempting to reduce God to make him more approachable on my terms.

This transcendent God must call the shots. God is so high that we could not make it to him. We were so low that the gospel was our only hope. This good news sounds so scandalous to us due to the unthinkable chasm Christ journeyed to reach down. God is not approachable on our terms, but he has approached us on his own. I'm overwhelmed at how great he is, but I'm undone by how he close he comes to one as small as me.

✂ **TRANSCENDENCE** REVIEW

Incorrect Perception: ~~God is the man upstairs~~.

Correct Attribute: *God is transcendent.*

Definition: *The transcendence of God means that he greatly surpasses our human worth and experience.*

Focal Verse: *For as the heavens are higher than the earth, so are my ways higher than your ways and my thoughts than your thoughts (Isa. 55:9).*

Implication: *God is too high to approach on our own terms so that our only hope is if he comes down to us.*

📄 **FURTHER** STUDY

What concepts from this chapter challenged you?

Meditate on Genesis 11:1-9. What does this passage teach us regarding man's attempt at transcendence?

As these builders worked really hard to construct an imposing building, what does the first verb associated with God in verse five tell us about God's position in relation to their highest efforts?

CORRECTIVE THEOLOGY

How does God's transcendence remedy our perspectives?

If God really is as great as Scriptures teach, how does that help you process how big your problems really are?

What personal issue is challenging your faith in God's transcendent ability?

CHAPTER 4
THE VIDEO SCREEN GOD

In every arena of our culture, we have grown more accustomed to viewing leaders speak to crowds from video screens. Preachers preach, teachers teach, trainers train, comedians entertain, doctors prescribe, and musicians inspire all from the convenience of a video screen. From the comfortable safety of our devices and the detached nature of their mediums, we have grown accustomed to receiving information without experiencing connection. While we can see the leader, we have this understanding that the leader can't see us. Even if the speaker had some type of video feed enabling him to watch us, we are guaranteed to be another number lost among the masses. Due to the height of the professional's popularity, we accept that there is a limited chance to ever become acquainted with the one who inspires us so definitively.

Somehow this approach sneaks into our theology. With the vast number of needs and the immense responsibilities that God has, we tend to think that he is too busy and we are too insignificant to gain an audience with him. Is God even concerned or aware of our present status?

Your inadequacies rob you of the notion that God even cares to notice your current situation. While you might accept that you show up on God's universal radar, you never imagine that you could show up on his refrigerator door. There are far too many interesting people for him to notice someone as inconsequential as you. You perceive God as displayed upon the screen of life providing answers, but you never anticipate that he will recognize you when you raise your hand with a question. Not only are we tragically incorrect regarding God's proximity to us, but we are significantly stifling the life God has planned for us. Neglecting the awareness of the presence of God leads to a joyless, purposeless existence. You must awaken to the reality that God is not detached from you. In fact, he sees you more clearly than you see him. If you could truly comprehend the truth that God desires intimacy with you more than you do with him, your soul would eagerly leap to a repositioned nearness.

God is not detached. God is immanent.

THE IMMANENCE OF GOD

The reason the attribute of immanence is so essential in our lives is that we have accepted an unhealthy sense of remoteness from God. Despite our preconceived notions, we do not serve a detached God with an arsenal of bodyguards protecting him within a gated community. He isn't trying to keep us out of his hair. We have yet to bother him enough where we have gotten on his nerves. We are not following a religious leader who isn't aware of the devoted followers lagging behind him. We aren't another insignificant need upon the ever-increasing deified to-do list. If the sparrows aren't forgotten by God (Luke 12:6), you can rest assured he has his eye on you whom he deems as superiorly more valuable than they (Matt. 6:26). You have never left his gaze.

The immanence of God means that he is intimately near to us. The Almighty is almightily closer to you right now than the pages of this book are to your fingertips. He knows you better than you know yourself, and yet he is still crazy about you. The term actually means "remaining in" creation. While some religions claim that the universe is an extension of God, the Bible teaches that it is separate from him. While God is outside of us, the stunning reality is that he is still desirous to be near to us. God is present but distinct among creation, and yet he has intentionally positioned himself to be shockingly accessible.

Some will see the immanence of God as a contradiction to his transcendence. How could God be so far above us and yet so near to us at the same time? What is impossible for man to understand is possible for God to provide! The glorious nature of God's relation to us is that he is so far above and yet so very near. While he is over all, he is also in all (Eph. 4:6). While he dwells upon high, he also resides with him who is low (Isa. 57:15). He is in heaven above and on the earth beneath – there is none like him (Deut. 4:39)!

The immanence of God is simply breathtaking when you consider the transcendence of God. You look amazed at the work of his fingers and stand spellbound by the trace of his heart. When you genuinely comprehend how such a transcendent God has come so immanently close, you can echo the psalmist who said, "When I look at your heavens, the work of your fingers, the moon and the stars, which you have set in place, what is man that you are mindful of him, and the son of man that you care for him?" (Ps. 8:3-4). He thinks of you. He cares for you. He is close to you. The most important being in the universe holds the most important things in your life as important to him!

God is not aloof to our situations or detached from our lives. He really does pay attention to us. God is intimately aware of our thoughts, uniquely understanding of our motives, and carefully involved in our circumstances. He cares about the big things, and he cares about the small stuff as well. It's a lie from the pits of hell that attempts to convince you that your problems are too inconsequential to bring before such a powerful God. God is the perfect Father who excels at carrying his children (Deut. 1:30-31), and his back never gets tired (Isa. 40:28). If it concerns his child, it concerns him.

From Genesis to Revelation, a common scriptural thread is the promise that God is with us. Creation itself is described in its beginning as the Spirit of God hovering over the face of the waters (Gen. 1:2). Not sending another to do his job, God created all things with his words, and yet one creation he personally formed by design and personally breathed into for life (Gen. 2:7). Adam and Eve experienced an intimate nearness to God that is breathtakingly unfathomable. They were so close to God that they knew what his footsteps sounded like as he would come to meet with them in the cool of the day (Gen. 3:8).

Due to their unruly desire to be God rather than to know God, they sinned and were expediently evicted from Eden. In that garden, they were previously allowed to experience the unhindered presence of God. After their sin, they could no longer enjoy that perfect perk. God placed a cherubim armed with a flaming sword as a reminder that his nearness had been severely rejected due to their sin (Gen. 3:24). At this critical juncture, the narrative of Scripture seeks to resolve the central issue of how to reenter the presence of God.

Throughout Scripture, God reveals his immanence in the fact that he speaks and acts among rebellious people of which there are numerous explicit reminders. As the great flood commences upon Noah, God is the one who shuts the door to the ark (Gen. 7:16). Amidst Abraham's journey, God doesn't send a message but actually delivers the message himself (Gen. 18:1). Amid Jacob's wandering, God initiates a wrestling match to leave a lasting mark upon him (Gen. 32:30). Throughout every stage of Joseph's suffering, the enduring hopeful refrain was that God was yet with him (Gen. 39:2, 3, 21).

The hope of the exodus was not in Moses' potential abilities but in God's promised presence (Exod. 3:12). This revered leader reached legendary status because he actually knew the LORD face to face (Exod. 33:11; Deut. 34:10). As Joshua stepped into Moses' massively sacred shoes, God graciously reassured him by promising the same presence that Moses experienced (Josh. 1:5, 9; 6:27). The reason why Samuel was a faithful priest (1 Sam. 3:19), the power that made David a brave warrior (1 Sam. 18:14), and the impetus for Hezekiah serving as a noble king (2 Kgs. 18:7) was because God was with each one of them. Walking through the valley of the shadow of death (Ps. 23:4), enduring through times of trouble (Ps. 46:1, 7, 11), and persevering through moments of need (Ps. 71:12) are all possible because the nearness of God is our good (Ps. 73:28).

As if his immanence in the Old Testament wasn't enough, God literally comes in the flesh in the opening pages of the New Testament. The presence of Jesus takes God's immanence to another level. Jesus' moniker was Immanuel which means "God with us" (Matt 1:23). The Word emptied himself to come near (Phil. 2:7) and became flesh to dwell among that which he created (John 1:14). Jesus promised his continual presence even as he ascended to the heavens and sent the disciples out for the nations (Matt. 28:20).

On the day of Pentecost, the Holy Spirit filled each of these disciples (Acts 2:4). As if God beside them through the person of Jesus wasn't enough, now God inside them through the person of the Holy Spirit would come and serve as their abundant advantage (John 16:7). As he guided these disciples on their missional way, the goal was leading them to heaven where mankind would finally experience an unhindered reunion with the dwelling place of God (Rev. 21:3). At that glorious return to Eden, we will no longer need a temple to remind us of God's presence because we will behold him at a stifling level of proximity (Rev. 21:22). We won't need any light to cascade upon his silhouette any longer, because his glory will be all the light we could ever need (Rev. 21:23). While sin separated us from the presence of God, the grand narrative of the Bible describes the work of Jesus as reuniting us back to God in Paradise.

God's presence is the most consistent force in the Scriptures and the most needed reality in our lives. The balm for the weary soul (Ps. 71:12), the justice for the disenfranchised outcast (Ps. 68:5), the courage for the overmatched warrior (Josh. 1:5), the comfort for the betrayed sufferer (Gen. 39:23), the power for the incompetent orator (Exod. 4:12), and the affirmation for the under-qualified servant (Acts 4:13) was all the same – the nearness of God. The greatest promise of God is the presence of God.

THE NEARNESS WE NEED

I have often found myself praying for the presence of God. Why would I pray for that which has already been promised? If the narrative of Scripture is chock full of reminders of God's continual presence, I need not ask for what I already have. My issue is not being granted God's presence but acknowledging it.

While God's immanence is a promised certainty, it can often feel like a fleeting encounter. If the presence of God is guaranteed, then why is the sense of his presence lacking? Every believer has experienced those wilderness type moments that frighten even the most stable of followers. Like barren ground craves a drop of water, all of us will suffer what seems like a drought of God's presence. Why does this happen? There's not one answer that resolves every situation, but there are specific categories to consider.

First, you could miss the presence of God due to unconfessed sin. We can't experience the presence of God fully when we treasure sin more deeply. In a believer's life, sin doesn't change one's status before God, but it does complicate one's relationship with God. God's presence doesn't demand moral perfection, but a callous heart (Eph. 4:19) ultimately disdains the nearness of God due to a more intense longing for sin. The psalmist declared that "if I had been aware of malice in my heart, the Lord would not have listened" (Ps. 66:18). A casual acceptance of the presence of sin without a desire to fight against it reveals an apathetic allowance for separation from the presence of God. You can't hide from the one who fills heaven and earth (Jer. 23:23-24), but you can foolishly try to ignore him by embracing sins of which he will not associate.

Second, you could experience distance due to incorrect doctrine. A failure to accept this transformational doctrine of God's immanence will result in divine distance. If you don't believe God to desire nearness with you, why would you ever anticipate experiencing it? God doesn't send a shepherd for us,; he becomes a shepherd to us (Ezek. 34:11, 15). Our God is near to us whenever we call upon him (Deut. 4:7). We are unable even to flee from his presence (Ps. 139:7). Refuse to accept the lie that God is distant.

Third, beware of the effects of troubling circumstances. Every trial will either bring you closer to God or further from God. Graciously, God dwells in the place where we need him most (Ps. 68:5-6). It is to our folly if we assume God's distance during times of trouble. In reality, his persistent presence is the only thing keeping us afloat. Instead of giving an annotated list of responses to suffering Job's questions, God instead gave him his presence (Job 38:1) to which Job's questions were forgotten and his mouth was covered (Job 40:4). Once Job had graduated from hearing about God to hearing from God himself (Job 42:5-6), his theology and perspective were instantaneously healed.

Fourth, many people suffer due to a sense of contented remoteness. You have unfortunately accepted that following God from a distance is the only option. You feel remote from God, and you have just gotten used to it. Don't follow Jesus at a distance like Peter did on the way to the cross (Matt. 26:58) – close enough to keep a pace but not near enough to behold his face. Too many of us have accepted that abiding intimacy is too far from our grasp. Like Saul, we attempt to develop our brilliant strategies, but we need to draw near to God before taking another step (1 Sam. 14:36). He is near, willing, and available.

Finally, it's difficult to experience the immanence of God when we give it a negligent effort. It's hard to get closer to God if we aren't making any attempts to do so. Just like a married couple can be seated physically beside one another and yet emotionally be in different timezones, God's presence is so readily available, but many of us aren't taking advantage of it. If we serve a God who wants you to call him "Father" when you pray (Luke 11:2), what does that mean about his willingness to connect? Draw near to God, and he will draw near to you (Jas. 4:8). Seek him with all your heart (Jer. 29:13) – not just some of your heart.

If you could be roused from your slumber just to realize his proximity and the power that reality brings, your life would change forever.

God is near. The nearness of God is your good. We should never grow accustomed to the fact that God Almighty desires to draw near to sinners like us. War against the belief that God should be honored that you are in his presence. When you attend a worship service, read your Bible, or pray to him, you are not the noteworthy participant. He is the one by whom we should be amazed. If and when we do acknowledge his presence, he is the honored guest and we are the blessed benefactors. Never get over the fact that the most glorious being in the entire universe desires to be near to you. You are not alone even at this moment. Glory is standing by, and he is near. God Almighty has drawn near not because anyone has forced him, but because he desires to come close. In his presence, your troubles may not go away, but they at least are refocused in a proper perspective.

✂ IMMANENCE REVIEW

Incorrect Perception: ~~God is detached from me~~.

Correct Attribute: *God is immanent.*

Definition: *The immanence of God means that he is intimately close to us.*

Focal Verse: *That they should seek God, in the hope that they might feel their way toward him and find him. Yet he is actually not far from each one of us (Acts 17:27).*

Implication: *God's presence is too close to permit loneliness any longer.*

📄 FURTHER STUDY

What ideas from this chapter comforted you?

Meditate on Psalm 139:1-18. What does this passage teach us about God's immanence?

If God knows you this close, what are some of the thoughts that he has about you (Ps. 139:17)?

📋 **CORRECTIVE** THEOLOGY

How does God's immanence impact the way you process your good and bad moments?

If God is still this close, knowing what he knows about you, what does that imply about his commitment to you?

How does God's nearness impact the moments that you feel alone?

CHAPTER 5
THE GERIATRIC GOD

When you picture God, what comes to your mind? For many people, they imagine a white-haired, bearded man who has obviously been around for quite some time. Throughout history, cultures have frequently depicted God as an older man who fits the ethnicity of the specific people creating the particular artwork. Typically arrayed in a white robe, his fabric even gives the appearance that his fashion sense is severely ancient.

Many people follow this Geriatric God. He's really, really old. God is the only being that you can honestly say is older than dirt. Depending upon your current age, you would define the threshold of when someone becomes geriatric differently than another person. Regardless of the classification of when an individual reaches senior status, it is inevitable that geriatrics slow down. Their bodies gradually show the wear and tear of decades lived on this planet. While children grow to a certain height, seniors will cite that they remembered a point where they began to shrink. While they can still do a lot at their age, they are unable to accomplish former tasks or complete them at their previous paces.

This perception of the Geriatric God adds multi-millennia to the typical elder disposition. We picture the older people in our lives as full of wisdom and yet overcome by frailty. People who believe God to be an ancient man respect him as an experienced sage with various positive and negative implications. By weathering such a long existence, we tend to perceive God as tired, taxed, and troubled. His age might be the reason he seems so out of date in our current culture. For such an old guy, he's doing rather quite well given the circumstances, but none of us knows how the coming years will impact his ability to do his job.

God is not geriatric. God is eternal.

THE ETERNALITY OF GOD

God is not old. He is eternal. The difference has massive implications. God is not a possessor of age because he is not bound by time. For God to have an age would imply that something is older than he. Nothing can be before God. God never had a start.

The eternality of God means that God exists outside of time. Being eternal, God has not been seasoned. He does not classify within the senior adult community. God is not older now than he was, and there was never a younger version of himself. He is as "young" now as he has ever been. There has never been a moment of eternity where God's presence was lacking, and yet, he has never aged a day. God is untouched by time, yet time is inevitably touched by God. God has never been new. God will never be old.

We have two options concerning time: either God is eternal, or the universe is eternal. Something had to be before all other things. If the universe is eternal, that means that some form of matter always existed or at least existed at the moment when nothing turned into something. In that view, you either have to hold that matter has been fundamentally eternal or its genesis is as far back as time can go and therefore, practically endless.

Or the other alternative is that someone outside of the universe began the universe within his eternal framework. He always existed, and at the right time, he commenced all that we know and see. What takes more faith? What view seems more outlandish? It appears more reasonable to me that an eternal God created the complex universe rather than that complex universe created itself by accident. The more you study the world, it seems to be screaming to us regarding the existence of an eternal God. As modern science develops, the discoveries

5: THE GERIATRIC GOD

seem to affirm theological positions originating in Genesis, Job, and Psalms. Some unthinkable catalyst powerfully initiated the universe then stopped it before it destroyed itself. Such a force must have divine fingerprints upon it.

God has always been. He is not full of days; he is the Ancient of Days (Dan. 7:9). There was never a moment that God did not exist. If he had an origin, he is a creation. God cannot be a creation. If he is anything less than the Creator, he is not God. He cannot be. With an origin point, that means that something is before him and strips away his status as God. The origin of God would imply that he had a beginning and therefore could and should have progression and improvement. If he can develop, he is not God.

While God's attribute of eternality is hard to comprehend, it is necessary to uphold. God was the beginning of all things (Gen. 1:1; John 1:3; Col. 1:16). It is commonly stated that God was in the beginning, but he was also the stimulant of the origin of all things. It is essential to realize that God did not predate Creation by a few minutes or a few years. If God is truly eternal, we must hold to a different reality. God existed eternity backward just as far as he will endure eternity forwards. If you rewind all the way back to the beginning of time, you still have an eternity of God's existence before the notion of Creation's existence. "The LORD is the everlasting God, the Creator of the ends of the earth" (Isa. 40:28).

Do you struggle to comprehend that concept of his eternality? Then you are finally starting to understand it. In our inability for comprehension, we see the essential nature of this attribute. God is entirely out of our league. The number of his years is unsearchable (Job 36:26).

God is *El Olam*. He is the "eternal God." Abraham, even in his geriatric age, referred to God as the everlasting one (Gen. 21:33). After waiting for what seemed like an eternity to have a son, God blessed Abraham with a baby boy. When Abraham was 100 years old, he became the most geriatric man to drop a child off at the nursery. How could such a miracle happen? Abraham understood that while he may have felt ancient, God was eternal. If God is eternal, what could be beyond his capability?

The account of Abraham is found in the early pages of Scripture. We see him first mentioned in Genesis 11 to be exact. If you are one of the faithful few that tries to maintain an understanding of the biblical timeline, you would understand that Abraham comes after Adam but before Aaron. You might know that Israel's first kings reigned in the order of Saul, David, and then Solomon. Joseph of the Old Testament predates Joseph of the New Testament. John the apostle comes after Jonah the prophet.

When you start to develop this framework, you are able to move forward and backward through the biblical timeline tracing our faith family tree. If you take a figure recorded in the early pages like Abraham and put him next to one of the later individuals like Barnabas, you realize that centuries separate them. The natural tendency is to think God is simply older than the oldest person in the Bible. As Paul is older than Timothy, Mary is older than Paul, Malachi is older than Mary, and so on. As you continue down the path, you arrive at Adam, the first created being. In a simple yet reasonable mindset, Adam's genesis must, therefore, be closer to God's genesis than say ours. Adam is closer in age to God than we are. And that idea is proof that we aren't thinking correctly. God has been around just as long before Adam as he was before Paul. God is not merely older than us. He is eternal.

The modern mind scoffs at such a notion. If there was a Creation, what was God doing for eternity? He had a life before us. God was busy even before all things were created. God "chose us in him before the foundation of the world, that we should be holy and blameless before him" (Eph. 1:4). The relationship between the eternal Father and the eternal Son existed before time even began. Jesus taught his disciples that he had received love from the Father even before the creation of the world (John 17:24). Not only was Jesus loved before time, but he was also "slain before the foundations of the world" (Rev. 13:8). How is that even possible? We can narrow down to the approximate year when Jesus was most likely crucified. That event wasn't that long ago historically speaking.

It wasn't that distant in our eyes, but the reality has existed forever in God's eyes. God can see every moment just as clearly as he sees this one. Time doesn't encapsulate God. Nothing limits him. He sees today's light as clearly as he sees the first light when he commanded it to be. In addition, there is not a future glimmer that fails to be in complete focus for him.

While we see today closely, remember yesterday vaguely, and anticipate tomorrow anxiously, God sees every single day of history as clearly as another. While each of those days have enough to overwhelm us, the eternity of God provides a grounding force for his children like no other. "Now to him who is able *to keep you from stumbling* and to present you blameless before the presence of his glory with great joy, to the only God, our Savior, through Jesus Christ our Lord, be glory, majesty, dominion, and authority, *before all time and now and forever*. Amen" (Jude 24-25). The fact that he is eternal means that we don't have to stumble. God's eternal nature is the stabilizing force that we so desperately need. He didn't need angels or men to provide him glory; he laid hold of it from eternity past!

Since God can see every day of eternity clearly, he is also able to process the events of today in context within the scope of eternity. Like the kayaker fighting through surging river currents unable to see anything other than the prevailing rapid, we can only process the present day's challenges. Yet from God's vantage point, he can see the current we made it through, the rapid in which we are currently struggling, and the tide around the bend of which we are still yet unaware. "The LORD is the true God; he is the living God and the everlasting King" (Jer. 10:10). As the only genuinely everlasting one, God is uniquely unsurprised by the present events, but he is also working among all of them and still holding fast to his plan because he sees eternity's entirety ever before him.

Since he keeps eternity in perspective, God will never rush. There is no need to hurry with God. He's never late. You can travel eternity back or eternity forwards, and you will never find a picture of a frantic God. Since he is not constrained by time, he will never spastically attempt to resolve his agenda. God alone actually inhabits eternity (Isa. 57:15). Why would he need to rush if he holds time in his hand untouched by it? A thousand years are like a day to him (Ps. 90:4; 2 Pet. 3:8).

THE INVULNERABILITY WE NEED

God is eternal, but I am not. I had a beginning. It wasn't too long ago, and I won't remain for too much longer. I am finite and vulnerable but not God. What grace I will be given if I am even able to live long enough to finish this book. I don't even know what tomorrow will bring. "What is your life? For you are a mist that appears for a little time and then vanishes" (Jas. 4:14).

As mist that is quickly extinguished by the slightest of efforts, my only viable hope is to grab ahold of something more secure than me. "Lord, you have been our dwelling place in all generations. Before the mountains were brought forth, or ever you had formed the earth and the world, from everlasting to everlasting you are God" (Ps. 90:1-2). There is a God in whom every generation upon the world has found its dwelling. God has been present with not only ancient generations past but promises to dwell with the future generations yet to come. From one far, unending edge of everlasting to the unthinkable, unreachable another edge of eternity, he is God. At every imagined side that we reach, we see we only have an eternity yet to travel further in before we reach it. With God, there are no edges to his existence or limitations to his life.

As one who has been around the block a few eternal times, shouldn't I trust him for my tomorrow? It is unthinkable how many times I ignore his help as if the security of eternity could be discovered within my finite frame. "O LORD, make me know my end and what is the measure of my days; let me know how fleeting I am!" (Ps. 39:4). My life is fleeting compared to his unlimited span. There is a precise measurement to my lifespan, but there has never been a ruler long enough to calibrate a mere fraction of his life. I serve towards an end for one who never saw a beginning. I am not eternal, but I have been invited into a relationship with the eternal one.

So while I am not eternal, my soul will live for eternity. I did have a specific starting point, but I will not have an ending point. Yes, this life will end one day, but my soul will live somewhere forever. Eternity past is unaccessible but eternity forward is unavoidable. Each one of us will live for eternity either enjoying the presence of Jesus or grieving the absence of Jesus. Eternity is God finally giving us what we have always wanted. For those who wanted him, they joyously enter into the glories of heaven. For those who have wanted for God to get his nose out of their business, God finally grants them their wish and instantaneously they realize their error of which they can ponder upon for eternity. Instead of eating from the tree of life, we each choose to eat from the tree of knowledge of good and evil (Gen. 2:9). Sin's wages are death (Rom. 6:23), so how will we live forever? How can we reenter into his presence?

To enjoy him for eternity, we must trust him for eternity. "Trust in the LORD forever, for the LORD GOD is an everlasting rock" (Isa. 26:4). Trusting God for eternity is what the gospel is all about. As a finite person, you must believe that the only eternal one provides the only way into a heavenly security. God is eternally holy. We are rebelliously sinful. Jesus was relentlessly committed. He would not allow any obstacle in his way from making it to the cross with our names upon it. On that tree, Jesus absorbed the full wrath of God deservedly marked for us. Trusting him as your substitute allows you to stand forgiven before a holy God so you can spend eternity swimming in the riches of all that he is. If eternity overwhelms you, realize that it will take that type of forever to investigate the infinite riches of the eternal God.

My temporal days should be spent in light of eternal realities.

My days have been determined and my time has been limited (Job 14:5). God has even written the last chapter of our lives before we have yet to read the first. Even more clearly than you can decipher these words on this page, God can behold the last pages of our lives as a reality in the here and now (Ps. 139:16). A God with such eternal knowledge deserves our trust. "So teach us to number our days that we may get a heart of wisdom" (Ps. 90:12). We are running out of time on this world. Are we making it count? Until I understand that this life is temporal, I won't live for things eternal. Live for that which outlives you. Use this day to remind yourself that you should live wisely in light of the eternal one who made you.

✂ ETERNALITY REVIEW

Incorrect Perception: ~~God is older than everyone else~~.

Correct Attribute: *God is eternal.*

Definition: *The eternality of God means that God exists outside of time.*

Focal Verse: *Before the mountains were brought forth, or ever you had formed the earth and the world, from everlasting got everlasting you are God (Ps. 90:2).*

Implication: *Don't waste a life given by an eternal God on temporal pursuits.*

🗐 FURTHER STUDY

What thoughts from this chapter made you think?

Meditate on Psalm 90:1-17. What does this passage teach us about God's eternality?

How does numbering our days in light of the eternality of God help us gain a heart of wisdom (Ps. 90:12)?

CORRECTIVE THEOLOGY

If God has processed all of history, how does he interpret current culture?

How should God's eternal perspective alter the way we process daily struggles?

What is required for us to live with God forever?

CHAPTER 6
THE UPGRADED GOD

We live in a digital world in need of constant updates and revisions. Every groundbreaking technological gadget is obsolete within a few mere months due to ever-changing upgrades. What once seemed sufficient and satisfactory becomes antiquated and outdated in no time. Books require revisions, software require updates, devices require enhancements, homes require renovations, and standards require amendments. We live in a world that assumes everything needs an upgrade.

Our culture seems to believe that God requires an upgrade as well. If he indeed is eternal, there must have been some type of progression along the way. The centuries of experience on his résumé make us believe that God must have advanced at different times, and we must now help him determine what revisions he currently needs to make to himself and his archaic methods. If God is to endure during our time, he is going to have to get up to speed with our progressive way of thinking and our manner of living. The only way he could have stayed necessary through the generations is if he worked hard to maintain relevance. Even if he used to think a certain way doesn't mean he still has to operate that same way now. We desire God to be up-to-date with the times. If he doesn't comply with our expectations, we will cut out what we don't like, copy something that scratches our itch, and paste it into our conglomeration of faith. Our culture is eagerly waiting for the next update that will relieve us from any unfortunate expectation coming from the previous model.

God does not need an upgrade. God is immutable.

THE IMMUTABILITY OF GOD

If God is perfect, there is no need for an upgrade. He has always been and will always be enough. The immutability of God is the only thing powerful enough to handle the constant changes in the world. It is the consistency needed to navigate this life as cultures continually modify throughout the centuries.

The immutability of God means that God is incapable of change. In a world specializing in inconsistency, God is unwaveringly consistent. He is the very standard of reliability. You never have to worry about whether God is in a bad mood or not when you approach him. God never has an off day. Think of how quickly our attitudes and demeanors can change. Consider how shifty our opinions are. Notice how rapidly someone can move from our good side to our bad side. We change constantly. God remains consistently.

God's immutability seems as if it is merely a lofty theological concept, but it also provides needed practical realities. Not only is God's immutability an impressive attribute, but this one grounds all the other attributes with abiding stability. How does this categorically play out regarding his identity and activity? God is unchanging in his person, purposes, promises, and passions.

First, God's person cannot be altered. Even the earth and the heavens will perish one day as they wear out like a garment (Ps. 102:25-26), but God is consistently the same (Ps. 102:27). For creation to change as much and as often as it does, the Creator must be changeless. Since his years have no end (Heb. 1:12), his demeanor in the future will remain consistent with what it has been in the past. God in the flesh is even categorized as being the same yesterday, today, and forever (Heb. 13:8).

God cannot alter from worse to better. If God can improve, he is not God. By his very nature, his character must be perfect without the possibility of enhancement in the slightest degree. If you compared our current reviews of God's conduct with the archives of Eden, you would discover that God has not improved in one way because you cannot improve perfection.

God cannot alter from better to worse. If God could change, we would inevitably be consumed (Mal. 3:6). If God possessed the potential for his character to deteriorate, the world would be thrust into unstable chaos. If an all-powerful God could plunge into all-encompassing evil, his nature would completely destroy creation. If he is susceptible to moral declination, he ceases to be God.

God cannot alter from this to that. Who he is today is who he will always be. With him, there is no variation or shadow due to change (Jas. 1:17). Only God can be God. If he is able to upgrade or downgrade, it precludes his ability to be God. The very nature of his identity must be synonymous with consistency. God is God - nothing less (because he would cease to be God) and nothing more (because there is nothing more significant than God).

Second, God's purposes cannot be adjusted. Every single one of God's promises to us is based upon "the unchangeable character of his purpose" (Heb. 6:17). God is not shifty. He's not going to make a plan today only to change it tomorrow. God is never going to encounter such intense opposition that he has to scramble to assemble a plan B. Once God established his plan, it will assuredly be accomplished. No one or nothing can stop him. "The counsel of the LORD stands forever" (Ps. 33:11). Since God is eternally holy, he can lay out a plan unworried if it will come to pass. "My counsel shall stand, and I will accomplish all my purpose" (Isa. 46:10).

All of our plans are subject to change, and that is why God's must not. If they changed, that meant he was unable to accomplish what he initially set out to do. It defies logic that God would establish a plan only later to discover he couldn't pull it off. If God's plan could benefit from a revision or update, the idea was not originally perfect, or the original planner was not perfect.

How have God's plans already come to pass? God has concretely purposed regarding Christ's appearing (John 17:5; 1 Pet. 2:20), our salvation (Eph. 1:4; 2 Tim. 2:19; Rev. 13:8), his wisdom (Matt. 13:35), the kingdom (Matt. 25:34), his agenda (Ps. 138:8), our inheritance (Eph. 1:11), and his grand redemptive plan (Eph. 3:9, 11). God has never picked up the newspaper and been surprised. No matter how hard we try to work against him, God stands untouched and unmoved while working among the creation to bring about his climactic redemptive conclusion.

Third, God's promises cannot be thwarted. "For all the promises of God find their yes in him" (2 Cor. 1:20). His promises to us can be trusted. There is no rebel of earth or devil of hell who can change our circumstances so much that God would be rendered unable to fulfill his promises to us. If God's words are true for a moment, they must be true for eternity. Even while everything within this earth will fade, "the word of our God will stand forever" (Isa. 40:8). If God has said it, it must come to pass. The standard of truth rests on the fact that God's promises are sure.

Due to his immutability, God cannot waver in his promises to his children or his enemies. If God has promised relief for his children, it will come at just the right time. If God has promised wrath for his enemies, it will come at precisely the right moment. "God is not man, that he should lie, or a son of man, that he should change his mind. Has he said, and will he not do it? Or has he spoken, and will he not fulfill it?" (Num. 23:19). His promises are so sure that we know "the Glory of Israel will not lie or have regret, for he is not a man, that he should have regret" (1 Sam. 15:29).

Fourth, God's passions cannot be manipulated. His manner implies reliability. God's sentiments are always perfectly stable and fair. You never have to worry if you are going to find God struggling to make it through a bad day. He is ever perfectly able to give the right response in the right way.

If God's emotions could be manipulated by another's, justice could never be accomplished. When the eternal judge lets the gavel fall, he must be confident that the sentence should last for eternity. "I am the LORD. I have spoken; it shall come to pass; I will do it. I will not go back; I will not spare; I will not relent; according to your ways and your deeds you will be judged" (Ezek. 24:14).

If he is immutable, why does he show grace then? The cross of Jesus proves God's perfect consistency regarding wrath and mercy. If God were a soft pushover with no standard of justice, he would let the thieves off the hook, but the bank account would still be depleted. If God were a hard tyrant, he would never allow such dangerous rebels like us dwell in his home forever. The cross of Christ displays both the grace and the wrath of God. Unable to bend on his standard of holiness, God allowed our sins to be paid for by a perfect sacrifice in Jesus. "It was to show his righteousness at the present time, so that he might be just and the justifier of the one who has faith in Jesus" (Rom. 3:26). At the cross, God revealed his unbending standard of justice upon Jesus and his unyielding desire for justification for us. Even in history's shocking salvific moments, God shows his immutability.

THE CONSISTENCY WE NEED

Consistency is one of the most challenging things to experience in our world. Our moods fluctuate. The weather defies logic. The team sure to claim victory collapses in defeat. As soon as we think we have something figured out, it changes again. That is why God's immutability is so pertinent for our souls. Within his character, we find the consistency that we need. He is the necessary steadying force within our lives. Since he cannot change, we know there is one thing in this universe upon which we can rely.

If God is immutable, how do we reconcile those times in Scripture when it appears that God changed his mind? Does the change of direction reveal that God is actually mutable? For if he has evolved in the past, that implies he could possibly change in the future. If we believe he has the propensity for change, then our efforts would move from submitting under his lordship to attempting to convince him the reasons why he should surrender to our desires.

When Scripture indicates God's change of direction, it is always preceded by another's positive or negative change. Every parent understands this dynamic. "If you hit your brother again, you will be punished…You are not going out this weekend if you fail to complete your homework…I am pulling this car over if you don't stop it." Depending upon how intimidating your parental demeanor is, your children may or may not comply. You respond inline with how they behave. It doesn't mean you change your mind. If they choose poorly, you will deliver punishment. If they return to their senses and do what has been asked of them, you are eager to withhold further discipline.

God is the same way. Throughout the pages of Scripture, God reveals how he processes the faithful and unfaithful decisions of his people. God communicated sorrow over his creation of mankind in the early stages of history (Gen. 6:6). The increasing nature of sin wasn't a surprise to God, but he was notably unfiltered to inform us that such blatant rebellion was legitimately offensive to him.

Sometimes the Bible does say that God changed his mind. What is happening in those moments? Moses prayed to spare the Israelites from God's judgment, and God listened (Exod. 32:9-14). God regretted making Saul king (1 Sam. 15:10). Hezekiah requested for longer life and received it (Isa. 38:1-6). God relented regarding Nineveh's previously promised destruction (Jonah 3:4, 10).

Did God actually change his mind or did his stance cause the individuals to change their mind? Regarding Moses, God was intentionally using that pivotal encounter to further develop a shepherd like heart into his leader (Exod. 32:32). God's regret over Saul wasn't an emerging realization because he warned them of such a tyrannical leader (1 Sam. 8:18). God's plan was for Hezekiah to have a longer life, and he intentionally planned for prayer to be part of the process for how that happened (2 Kgs. 20:5-6). Nineveh actually did what God required of them, and so he was eager to show more mercy to them than the prophet was (Jonah 4:11).

God's changeless dispositions respond to others' changing directions.

Nothing takes him by surprise, but as the Creator, his purposes do include responding to the decisions of the creation. If you cross the line he said not to pass, he is going to deliver the promised punishment. If you are willing to alter a previously charted course due to his warning, he is eager to reward your prudent adjustments. God is decidedly moving forward with his plan while rewarding our decisions.

God's plans include prayers as a part of his process and purpose. When God uses prayer as part of the proceedings, it is meant to involve us but not depend upon us. The greatest thing that prayer changes is us. As we ask the immutable God to act, we are reminding ourselves that we aren't in charge. That's part of his eternal plan!

If God doesn't change his mind, what about his emotions? Throughout Scripture, it seems as if God has impassioned shifts. Never fear – God's emotional reactions are always consistent with his immutable character. Theologians disagree regarding God's passions. Some will claim that God is impassible claiming that he is without emotions. Others will argue that he has feelings but is not driven by their sway. While using anthropomorphic language, the Bible unashamedly attributes emotions to God. Using words with which we can understand and relate, the Bible describes God as showing deep sentiments. God feels joy (Isa. 62:5), grief (Ps. 78:40; Eph. 4:30), wrath (Exod. 32:10), pity (Ps. 103:13), and love (Isa. 54:8; Ps. 103:17) just to name a few.

While the Bible sees no issue depicting God as possessing emotions, you never see his reactions determining his actions. He leads his emotions, but his emotions never lead him. God's emotional displays never compromise his sinless integrity. His anger is never so hot that it is unreasonable. His love is never so soft that he bends regarding his standards. God is not rendered helpless by his emotions, but he apparently does have them. Do you understand the positive ramifications that God can be provoked to some level of an emotional response due to his commitment with those he created? While I would be scared to death of a God who could be manipulated by human tears, petition letters, or reasonable ultimatums, I also don't see the Bible depicting a God who is indifferent to our decisions.

If God were a mere machine that stoically delivered a grade by our penciled-in bubble answers from our submitted tests, we would be stuck in a stuffy religious system rather than a vibrant relational covenant. God does reveal and respond, and yet he is unchanging. He never compromises his unwavering reliability. That's the only way our unreliable souls can endure. Despite our ever-changing ways, he remains changeless. You can forever depend upon his consistency. If everything else changes, our God remains reliably immutable.

✂ IMMUTABILITY REVIEW

Incorrect Perception: ~~God requires updating to stay relevant~~.

Correct Attribute: *God is immutable.*

Definition: *The immutability of God means that God is incapable of change.*

Focal Verse: *For I the LORD do not change; therefore you, O children of Jacob, are not consumed (Mal. 3:6).*

Implication: *God is mesmerizingly consistent, so you never have to fear him changing on you.*

📄 FURTHER STUDY

What concepts from this chapter encouraged you?

Study Psalm 102:25-28. How does this passage compare the Creator to his creation?

How does God's immutability allow us to dwell secure (Ps. 102:28)?

CORRECTIVE THEOLOGY

How are we to process God's immutable nature against the culture's changing narratives?

Regarding God's immutability, what traits or promises of God are you most thankful are incapable of changing?

How does God's consistent presence in your life encourage you based upon your experiences with other people?

CHAPTER 7

THE LITTLE ENGINE THAT COULD GOD

"I think I can. I think I can. I think I can."

We all remember this iconic phrase from the children's classic *The Little Engine That Could*. This beloved tale recounts the story of a determined train hauling toys up the mountain to some needy children. When the train is unable to make the steep trek, the toys try to chorale other passing locomotives to carry them up to the top of the mountain. Either due to disinterest or inability, all the trains refuse the responsibility of hauling this load. Eventually, a little blue engine comes by who is unsure if it can pull such a weight up the mountain. Seeing the disappointment in the eyes of the toys, the engine decides to give it a shot. Repeating that famous phrase over and over again, this little locomotive eventually musters up enough strength to help out those in need.

Many of us follow The Little Engine That Could God. No one would readily admit it, but we prove it by our actions. When encountering difficult situations in our lives with what seems to be insurmountable odds, we look for the best and the brightest to come to our rescue. We seek direction from doctors, teachers, preachers, counselors, and every expert you can imagine. Once we exhaust all of our human resources and have made meager attempts of our own, we address the King of kings and Lord of lords and utter one of the most tragic phrases resonating in our churches today, "All we have left to do now is pray." Maybe, just maybe, if we can assemble enough people to pray together in the right way, we can provide God with the needed strength for the impending obstacle. We think he can. We think he can. We think we can.

God has become our second string desperation rather than our first string guarantee. He has become a last ditch effort rather than the only valid option. Our circumstances cause us to render God helpless in our minds, and we try to obtain results on our own.

God is not the Little Engine That Could. God is omnipotent.

THE OMNIPOTENCE OF GOD

Does God have the power to do all things? Is God limited or restricted by anything? For certain events to come to pass, does God require our prayers, help, or involvement? The manner in which you answer each of those questions reveal much concerning your theology.

The omnipotence of God means that God is all-powerful. His unlimited ability cannot be hindered by anyone or anything in this world. He can do whatever he wants whenever he wants to do it. No challenger threatens to usurp him. The type of dualism that pits a supremely good force against a supremely evil force duking it out over the centuries is not even close to reality. The most powerful individuals and institutions are hopelessly unmatched with the God of the Bible.

Not only is his power unstoppable, but he also utilizes that power effortlessly. He never tires out. An avid athlete maintains a particular physique by consistently running a certain distance that is manageable for him or her. If pushed, the challenging marathon might be within reach, but the effort would leave the runner depleted for some time afterward. Needing recovery, the runner would learn over the next few days that even though he or she crossed the finish line, the runner's body paid for it. This athletic example is not congruent with God's ability. Nothing stretches the muscles of God. The act of recreating the heavens and the earth when Christ returns is no more taxing on God than when he sends one tiny raindrop upon a single dandelion. In either case, he never even breaks a sweat. God's unlimited power puts him in a category all by himself. He is not merely a god; he is Almighty God.

The older we get, the more our theology requires rehab. As a young child, we stand in awe of a God who set the stars in their place. We have no problem understanding him to be powerful enough to handle any situation. Adulthood seeks to rob our faith by tempting us to trust ourselves. As the years go by, we tend to rely more on our own disillusioned abilities than upon the unlimited power of the Omnipotent God.

I can still remember the time when God met that great financial need in my life. I am unable to forget the time he rescued my friend from the bonds of addiction. I can still see the doctor's expression when she saw that little boy walk in her office who was never supposed to stand on his feet. I can remember those pivotal moments when I watched God make the impossible possible, but oh, how I forget them when a new set of obstacles come my way! The fact that the moments when God does something spectacular among us is still astonishing to us reveals that we do not fully comprehend who we are dealing with here. We become like the father whose son is demon-possessed. Exhausted by all his failed efforts at acquiring deliverance for his son, he insufficiently implores Jesus, "If you can do anything, have compassion on us and help us" (Mark 9:22).

Jesus replied, "If you can? Everything is possible to the one who believes" (Mark 9:23). This man looks at the Messiah only to caution him that they have tried everything in their own power and nothing has worked so far. Jesus is the last resort, and if he can help, they would surely appreciate it. Can you imagine the look in Jesus' eyes? Can you think about what his voice sounded like when he thundered his response, "If you can?" All we have to do today is look back over our shoulders and realize that God is not in heaven looking at our current situations chanting, "I think I can. I think I can. I think I can."

Our lack of faith robs us of seeing Jesus work miraculously in our lives. We need to respond honestly like that father did, "I do believe! Help my unbelief" (Mark 9:24). Out of all the faith statements in the Bible, I believe this response to be one of the most genuine and essential. He acknowledged that his faith was incomplete, but he at least portrayed a proper perspective. Even when your faith is underdeveloped, don't allow it to be misdirected.

As frail humans, we learn that many things are impossible for us, but those moments invite us to realize that with God all things are possible (Matt. 19:26). In fact, "nothing will be impossible with God" (Luke 1:37). He can do all things, and it is impossible for a single purpose of his to be thwarted by another (Job 42:2). God is great and abundant in power (Ps. 147:5), and nothing is too difficult for him (Jer. 32:17). We ask for great things from such a great God, only to realize that he "is able to do far more abundantly than all that we ask or think, according to the power at work within us" (Eph. 3:20). Can that possibly be true? I make some bold requests, and I entertain some lofty concepts. Is he actually able to do more, not of just of what I can do, but of what I can imagine?

He can do all that and much more because his power is eternal and unlimited (Rom. 1:20) instead of temporal and limited like mine. When the Spirit of God comes, he comes in power abundantly able to embolden his people for any assignment (Acts 1:8). No problematic task is beyond God's scope. He not only can guarantee his plan's success but also the timing of its completion (Gen. 18:14). Compared to his omnipotent power, "all the inhabitants of the earth are accounted as nothing, and he does according to his will among the host of heaven and among the inhabitants of earth; and no one can stay his hand or say to him, 'What have you done?'" (Dan. 4:35). The Lord God is the Alpha and the Omega, the one "who is and who was and who is to come, the Almighty" (Rev. 1:8).

THE POWER WE NEED

When we are confronted with the reminders of our limited power, we attempt to disregard reality. As confident individualists, we want to prove to anyone watching that we can fix whatever is wrong. Relying on our feeble strength is not power but weakness. In God, we discover the power that we really need. Our frustrating frailty is a God-given, gracious invitation to behold his unique and matchless omnipotence.

In Matthew 14, the Gospel author reports on Jesus feeding the five thousand. After hearing about John the Baptist's death, Jesus attempted to separate himself from the crowd to grieve (Matt. 14:13). Due to the miracles Jesus had been performing, and the masses that accompanied them, he couldn't even find a brief moment to lament. As soon as he removed himself from the crowd by traveling in a boat, the people caught up to him on foot (Matt. 14:13). When Jesus disembarked from the vessel, the people were eagerly awaiting his arrival upon the shore. Tired and emotionally exhausted, Jesus peered into the people's needy eyes and chose to do something. He began to heal the sick and teach the people because they appeared to him like sheep without a shepherd (Mark 6:34).

As he ministered to the people, the hour became evening. In the hope of getting a break, the disciples encouraged Jesus to send the people away so they can get some rest and some food from some other place (Matt. 14:15). The disciples obviously didn't envision Jesus meeting this need because they had already polled the crowd to see if any food was available among the masses. It wasn't even on their collective radar that Jesus could address this need. Like those disciples, how often do we fail to miss that God is going to do something great in our midst because we are focused solely upon what others can't do?

Instead of sending the people away, Jesus instructed the disciples to give them something to eat. Among the whole crowd, the only food they discovered was from one boy's lunchbox. The disciple Andrew brought up this young boy to Jesus and offered his lunch to see what Jesus could do with it (John 6:8). This boy brought five loaves and two fish (Matt. 14:16). A Jewish loaf at this time would only feed about three people. Jesus took the food, got everyone to sit down on the green grass (cf. Ps. 23:2), gave a blessing, divided up the food, and gave it to the disciples in portions.

The Scripture says that all the people ate and were satisfied (Matt. 14:20). With 5,000 men, accompanied by their wives and children eating this meal, it is safe to assume that the crowd's size could have quadrupled leading the whole picnic party to equal approximately 20,000 people. Not only did they all eat, but they had twelve baskets full of leftovers. Can you imagine that little boy going home with all those to-go boxes full of food? His mom probably grounded him for his apparent outlandish lies!

The most tragic element of this story is what happens one chapter later. If you turn the page in the Bible, you might think you are reading a typo, but you unfortunately are not. In Matthew 14, Jesus feeds the 5,000, but in Matthew 15, he feeds the 4,000. This heading isn't a blunder, and the story isn't repeated. These two separate instances reveal the problem with our spiritual condition: we quickly forget how great our God is.

During the second occurrence, Jesus' life-changing teaching kept people glued to his every word for three days. At that moment, the disciples didn't ask Jesus to send the people away, Jesus rallied the disciples together because he was worried that if he sent them home, they might actually faint along the way due to the lack of nourishment (Matt. 15:32). This situation is more critical than the last similar incident.

At that particular occasion, Jesus made them aware of the need and waited to see how they would respond. The disciples looked the King of kings and Lord of lords in the eyes and asked him, "Where are we to get enough bread in such a desolate place to feed so great a crowd?" (Matt. 15:33). They were looking right at the source! Had they already forgotten? Did they have short-term memory loss? Did they forget to whom they were talking? What a telling portrayal of our resistance to accepting God's omnipotence!

What makes matters worse is that the details were stacked more in their favor on this second occasion. The disciples had already acquired seven loaves and a few fish (Matt. 15:34). Matthew doesn't record how many fish, but a few is at least more than two (which is more than last time). Jesus offered a blessing, commissioned the disciples to hand out the food, and they collected seven baskets full of leftovers (Matt. 15:37). This basket is not a small hand basket like the previous event, these baskets were the size of a hamper and the same type of basket able to fit a grown man like Paul when he was lowered in one to escape an angry mob (Acts 9:25). As before, women and children also ate and were satisfied, which probably brings the number to 16,000 people. They had previously seen God do more with fewer resources, and, confronted by a new set of obstacles, they were faithless in Jesus' ability to handle the situation.

Do you acknowledge the tragedy between these two events? They forgot how big God was. These disciples had developed spiritual amnesia.

Spiritual amnesia is a dangerous condition of fearing the present situation by forgetting the past deliverance.

As I read the accounts, it baffles me how anyone could experience God's omnipotent power yesterday only to forget about it tomorrow, until I realize that I do the same thing. The skepticism of the disciples must have been contagious to our own faith as well. We underestimate who we are dealing with here. God is all-powerful. He is rid of every ounce of anxiety regarding current circumstances or future challenges.

A quick trek down memory lane would remind you of his power in your life and through the pages of Scripture. When you remember what God has already done, it allows you to anticipate what he is about to do. Look over at the leftovers in the corner and let it remind you of the Omnipotent God who can take care of the next meal as well. What could possibly be stacked against you right now that your God could not handle? Failure to anticipate God's ability to address your circumstances makes more of a statement of your perception of God than it does a perception of your challenges.

He has the power to do it. Whatever it is, he can do it. No doctor's diagnosis has ever crippled this Healer. No dire need has ever stifled this Provider. No relational drama has ever confounded this Counselor. He excels in making the impossible possible. He is not struggling to make it up to the summit to reach his needy children. I imagine your circumstances are great, but our God is greater! The situation that overwhelms you is overwhelmed by your God. He is massively superior to your most significant conflict. Our God has all the power that you need. Instead of giving it to you, he will provide it for you.

✂ OMNIPOTENCE REVIEW

Incorrect Perception: ~~God requires our help in some situations.~~

Correct Belief: *God is omnipotent.*

Definition: *The omnipotence of God means that God is all-powerful.*

Focal Verse: *Ah, Lord GOD! It is you who have made the heavens and the earth by your great power and by your outstretched arm! Nothing is too hard for you (Jer. 32:17).*

Implication: *You can rest in the fact that God has enough power to do what he has promised he will do.*

🗐 FURTHER STUDY

What specific thought from this chapter challenged you?

Meditate on Mark 9:14-29. Watch for how this narrative compares the ability of Jesus compared to the inability of the disciples. What phrases stick out to you?

Look at the description of the disciples (Mark 9:18) and Jesus' instruction to them later (Mark 9:29). What does this reveal about the reason for the disciples' failure?

📋 **CORRECTIVE** THEOLOGY

What current challenges do you have that seem insurmountable?

In what powerful ways have you seen God move in the past?

How does God's activity in the past ground you for the challenges in the present?

CHAPTER 8
THE OVERBOOKED GOD

Have you ever tried to get an appointment with that really busy person? You keep trying to squeeze in a slot on the calendar, but you can never get him or her to lock into a time. Like the doctor that schedules an appointment months out or the friend who keeps promising to get together yet consistently fails to deliver, some people just seem untouchable because of their high demands. With busy businesses, you either endure that type of treatment, or you find a replacement for their services. With relationships, you begin to question if the schedule is really that tight or if the connection is really that dispensable. Maybe that overbooked schedule actually represents a disinterested relationship. Insecurities invade, and you can't help but wonder if this overbooked person is even willing to make an attempt to connect.

Many people view God in the same way. They tend to believe that God is so busy that he is only able to focus on one person or a few people at one time. If that is the case, many people feel as if their situation isn't critical enough to garner his attention. Just by the sheer nature of his occupation, God's schedule must surely be overbooked. To try to fit onto his calendar would probably leave you more than just a few months out. With all the pressing situations and impressive people out there, surely God's schedule must be full with more earth-shattering agendas than the ones we would annoyingly distract him with. If God is only going to attend to the most urgent situations, it is really doubtful to imagine that he is checking in on mine. I just doubt if I am really that important to him.

God is not overbooked. God is omnipresent.

THE OMNIPRESENCE OF GOD

God is not limited to being present in one place at one time. He is not regulated to interacting with only one person at one time. He is presently all-present. While his presence is not one with the entire universe, it is available for the whole world at the same moment. God's schedule is not overbooked, and his presence cannot be overlooked. His omnipresence guarantees our ability to access him at all times.

The omnipresence of God means that God is everywhere at every time. While such an infinite concept is difficult for finite minds to comprehend, is it true? How does that change our perception of God? For God to be all-present, there is no corner of the universe that his presence does not inhabit.

There is not a place where God is more present than another. God's presence is just as real in a church sanctuary as it is in a prison cell. He is in proximity to the pastor as close as he is to the prostitute. Work has never once kept him from his child's recital. He has never neglected the people in the room due to his attention to the people on the phone. Anxious concerns have never left him detached. Responsibilities never rendered him tardy even to that tragic situation. Preoccupation has never kept him estranged from his children. God has been there, he is there, and he will be there through it all.

In the joyful moments, we often overlook his pervading presence. In the sorrowful moments, we often blame his apparent absence. If he genuinely is omnipresent, he is there for every single one of those moments. He is celebrating alongside the new birth and grieving beside the stillbirth. God is present at the wedding altar as well as the divorce hearing. He oversees both the first service at the church plant as well as the last lockup at the church closing. God is close enough to behold the expressions when the repentant sinner receives the gospel as well as when the rich young ruler walks away. He doesn't miss a single second of any encounter. Even when a tree falls in an empty forest, it does not escape his notice.

God's omnipresence is highlighted immediately after Creation's completion. After all that God had made among the heavens and the earth, he was omnipresently able to "see all that he had made" at once (Gen. 1:31). After "the heavens and the earth were completed in all their vast array" (Gen. 2:1), he could observe it all in a single moment. If this God could simultaneously behold the most unique aquatic animal at the ocean's darkest depth all the while viewing the furthest constellation that the most advanced telescope could never reach, what makes us think that he couldn't also be present with Adam in those initial moments? How could you fathom that he wouldn't be right there with you right now?

One way to determine if you believe in the omnipresence of God is to articulate his capacity for collecting information at one time. Is he actually aware of all things at all times? Imagine you had a room full of people who all filled out the following line:

God, my favorite name for you is _____.

After selecting your preferred name, prepare all those in attendance to read their answers out loud after your verbal countdown. As the read-aloud commences, the sentence will sound incredibly unifying until each person reaches the last word. To your ears, it will sound chaotic, but how would it resonate in the ears of God? If everyone read the line at the same time, how many of those names could God hear, how many titles could he match with the person who spoke it, and how well could he process all that was said in his direction? To hold the belief in God's omnipresence, you must maintain that he understood everything clearly all at the same time. He can attribute every answer to each person and also knows the sincerity by which each mouth said it. Amazingly, comprehension would not be a challenge to him.

If that seems overwhelming to you, realize that you just imagined a scenario with only one room containing a few people. Now zoom out to the level if every church in your city did the same experiment at the same time. His signal is still unimpeded. Open it up to every person living on the planet right now. God still isn't straining to connect all the dots. You can take every person who has ever lived and invite them to complete the same exercise at the same time in different languages with varying levels of authenticity, and God could still place every single word in its proper context.

God's presence is not restricted to one place at one time. It is incorrect to think that God only dwells in certain areas and with certain people. King Solomon built a temple so glorious, yet this wise man understood what his structure could never seek to accomplish. "Heaven and the highest heaven cannot contain you; how much less this house that I have built!" (1 Kgs. 8:27). If the heavens are unable to contain God, neither can a meager building we construct. No matter how glorious an attempt at religious architecture might prove to be, it still falls short at representing or containing the glorious God.

While heaven is God's throne, he surprisingly looks upon even the humble and contrite (Isa. 66:1-2). He isn't contained by impressive structures, but he isn't standoffish by meager vessels either. A belief in God's omnipresence ensures that he is not insulated from any part of humanity. In him, all things hold together (Col. 1:17), but he "does not dwell in houses made by hands" (Acts 7:48). To restrict God's presence to houses of worship is a silly attempt to box him into a flawed man-made structure regardless of how ornate it is. While the gathering of God's people often proves to be unique, the building is never the secret stimulant. It is God's presence with me worshiping alongside God's presence with you that makes his presence often seem more strikingly tangible. An array of stones cannot compete with a gathering of people. God's presence is meant to dwell within sacred people more than among sacred places.

God's presence is available at all places at the same time. There is not a person to which God is closer than another. Some people might be more aware of God's presence, but that does not mean that a spiritual ranking exists separating the religious elite from the unimpressive common. No class, race, or gender has a monopoly on God's presence.

We are unable to flee from the presence of his Spirit because he is everywhere (Ps. 139:7-10). If God is both near and far at the same time as he fills both heaven and earth, there is nowhere we can hide from him (Jer. 23:23-24). As we begin to seek God, we realize that "he is actually not far from each one of us" (Acts 17:27). "Behold, to the

LORD your God belong heaven and the heaven of heavens, the earth with all that is in it" (Deut. 10:14). God is close to everywhere all the time. Attempting an escape from his presence is futile.

While God's presence is available to all at every moment, God's presence does not emanate a consistent demeanor with all people at the same time. The presence of God can evoke fear or calm depending upon one's spiritual condition. When the prophet Obadiah confronted Edom, he spoke concerning the day of the LORD being near upon all the nations (Obad. 1:15). He prophesied of a day when God would humble the Edomites on Mount Esau and exalt the Israelites on Mount Zion. God planned to work with two different people in two different ways at the same time. Some may see this ability as transferable to us. Surely a parent can be pleased with one child's decision and frustrated with another child's action. The difference is we are unable to divorce our feelings from our responses. If we are mad at an individual, we are altogether mad. Our demeanor cannot shift in a single moment. God can respond differently yet simultaneously to all people. God can keep his people as the flame yet while his enemies are the stubble (Obad. 1:18). The capacity to do both at the same time does not contradict his character or challenge his ability.

God's presence is always available, yet our connection is hindered due to our sin. We are like the first rebels separated from God. As soon as Adam and Eve first naughtily nibbled upon the forbidden fruit, the immediate reaction was to run and hide. They covered their newfound shame of nakedness with fig leaves and "hid themselves from the presence of the LORD God among the trees of the garden" (Gen. 3:8).

As God approached them in the cool of the day, they could discern his footsteps which made their position evermore telling. They used to anticipate jubilantly the sound of God coming near, but now, their sin had caused them to respond differently to the same consistent person. God called out to Adam and asked, "Where are you?" (Gen. 3:9). If God has the power to create all things with the power of his words, it is doubtful that he was unable to hone in on Adam's physical location at that point. God was asking a spiritual question and not a logistical question. God never lost Adam, but Adam lost Adam (Gen. 3:9). Our sins alienate us from God. "Your iniquities have made a separation between you and your God, and your sins have hidden his face from you so that he does not hear" (Isa. 59:2). In sin, we alienate ourselves from the life of God because of sheer ignorance (Eph. 4:18). Yet instead of leaving us alone in the darkness, he still comes looking for us!

THE AVAILABILITY WE NEED

If God's omnipresence is a reality, that implies that he is never overbooked. God will never reach such an overwhelming workload that he is unable to be present with us. For all the people who failed to come through when we needed them, God establishes the availability that we have always longed for someone to provide.

God's presence often feels lacking due to our unawareness. The issue is not that God is absent, but we are. We are too disconnected and apparently too disinterested to narrow the gap. Each of us has known someone who was physically present but emotionally absent. When we fail to seek the presence of God, we are accepting a sense of divine remoteness that is utterly unnecessary. Not only is it tragically inaccurate to believe God is distant from us, but it is also fundamentally dangerous to our spiritual condition.

Too often do we ask God to be with us. We need not pray for the presence of God for which we have already been promised. He guaranteed to be with us to the end of the age (Matt. 28:20). The LORD is the one "who goes before you. He will be with you; he will not leave you or forsake you. Do not fear or be dismayed" (Deut. 31:8). We serve a God who promises to be with us wherever we go (Josh. 1:9). When Jacob had a dream about a ladder coming from heaven, he awoke amazed. He said, "Surely the LORD is in this place, and I did not know it" (Gen. 28:16). Notice that the ladder was not for Jacob to go up, but for heaven to come down. God's presence was coming to Jacob. God is always present; we are just unaware. We need to pray for God to stir our awareness of his consistent presence.

Not only is God's presence readily available to all people, but God's presence is also tangibly accessible for all churches. We often categorize churches as those with which we can experience God's presence from those we cannot. As if some congregations are able to capitalize more on God's schedule than others, we divide local churches into a spiritual hierarchy. God does not withhold his presence from any group of yearning people. The unique experiences that seem more connected to God's presence have more to do with our sincere focus than God's apparent willingness. Scripture promises that God's presence brings peace and is present in all the churches composed of true saints (1 Cor. 14:33). As Jesus spoke to the seven churches in Revelation, he was present with each congregation and gave a specific message tailored to each one (Revelation 2-3). It wasn't a manufactured response regurgitated to each city. He had a distinct and fresh word for each unique context. God is never more present with one church over the other. God might be more pleased with one church over another, but that doesn't mean he isn't present with both.

God's presence guarantees his complete attention on you at all times.

He has never been distracted from one of his children. God is fully present and probably carrying you through more right now than you can possibly imagine (Deut. 1:30-31). Even though he has numerous children, God is not limited to care for one of his children at a time. The fullness of God's attention dwells on the entire creation at every single moment. What life-altering, universe-bending news! His availability should be a paradigm shift for your perspective. For in his presence, there is fullness of joy (Ps. 16:11). Every believer has been filled in him (Col. 2:9-10). That precious truth means that none of us have more access or restriction than another believer. He is present, aware, and available. God is never too overbooked to be present with you when you desperately need him or when you simply want him.

While we gravitate towards self-absorption, we might feel guilty if we knew that God's attention on us caused him to miss a brother or sister in need. No worries! That's where God's immanence (he is near) finds an infinitude in his omnipresence (he is near to all). As he is close to all the brokenhearted at the same moment (Ps. 34:18), I never have to worry that his attention on me means he is forced to neglect another. What a present Father we have! God is never too busy for his child.

✂ OMNIPRESENCE REVIEW

Incorrect Perception: ~~God is overbooked~~.

Correct Attribute: *God is omnipresent.*

Definition: *The omnipresence of God means that God is everywhere at every time.*

Focal Verse: *The eyes of the LORD are in every place, keeping watch on the evil and the good (Prov. 15:3).*

Implication: *God's omnipresence ensures that he has his complete attention on me at all times.*

🗐 FURTHER STUDY

What thoughts from this chapter stretched your thinking?

Meditate on Psalm 139:7-18. What does this passage teach us regarding God's omnipresence?

Out of all of God's responsibilities, how does it impact you regarding the intimate nature of his attention on you?

 CORRECTIVE THEOLOGY

Why do you struggle to believe that God is very much available to you right now?

While you can't be everywhere at one time, how should your belief in God's omnipresence alter your prayer life as you intercede for others?

As you recognize God's availability to you at this moment, what do you need to share with him? What do you need to remember about him?

CHAPTER 9
THE UNDERGRADUATE GOD

As students launch into their college careers, many are initially unsure regarding their desired outcome. Beginning with general electives, they start to sort through new information and slowly narrow down a focus to declare a major. After completion, these new alums are informed by graduate schools or potential employers that further learning is still required. Many lines of work expect ongoing education and occasional recertification. This seemingly never-ending quest for understanding always reminds us that complete knowledge has been and forever will be unfortunately out of our grasp.

Many people perceive God as being enrolled in the universe's undergraduate program. As time progresses, more knowledge is required of God. The cultural lessons are changing too rapidly for such an ancient God to maintain sufficient expertise in all areas. He is called upon assuming that he is a miracle-working oncologist, mild-mannered family counselor, level-headed financial adviser, grace-giving judge, and so many more multi-faceted specialized positions. For all the purposes for which he is called, there should be no way possible that he could serve as the universe's expert of more than a couple of areas.

Such a deity would require us to inform him continually of the updated information as our culture progresses. Not only is the knowledge needed to run the world expansive, but there is also much to know regarding the complexities of each individual person. Different personalities, ages, sexes, cultures, and backgrounds make people such secret keeping vaults that there is no feasible way that God could know it all. Surely there must be areas where he is ignorant. Maybe we have built the castle walls of our minds so high that he can no longer invade. With all that there is to know out there in the complex universe and the intricate mind of every person, God must still be enrolled in the university's undergraduate program with much more he needs to discover along the way. Over time, maybe he will reach a satisfactory level of comprehension under our extraordinary tutelage. With our help, he can hopefully increase his knowledge and potentially operate the affairs of the world from a more informed position.

God is not an undergraduate. God is omniscient.

THE OMNISCIENCE OF GOD

How much does God know? Is God's understanding increasing as the centuries progress? Does the universe have riddles for which God does not yet know the answer? The attribute regarding God's capacity for knowledge is foundationally vital to how we approach him.

The attribute of omniscience means that God is all-knowing. He is perfectly knowledgable about all there is to know. Nothing is hidden from God, and he has never known more or less than what he knows at this very moment.

God is not partial in his knowledge or incomplete in his understanding. Since God's very nature is unlimited, it implies that he would have to be infinite in his knowledge. If God could learn anything, he would not be God. If we could surprise him with some piece of information, he could not be God. He is not even dependent upon a progressive unveiling of history to collect data. God sees the end and the start as clearly as he sees the here and the now.

There is an endless amount of knowledge for God to know, so how does his omniscience interact with history? We are unable to understand what God knows, but it is essential to know that he actually knows it. While there are many facets to unpack regarding God's omniscience, there are a few significant points to consider.

First, God has complete knowledge regarding himself. If that seems like an easy feat, you are failing to acknowledge who we are dealing with here. Trying to know all there is about God is like spending your entire life reading a collection of material on a particular subject to become proficient in it only to find out in the end that you are still just on the title page. When it comes to God, we will get lost in all there is just to know about him. Regarding theology, it is not that the textbook continues to get revisions but that the content is just too vast. The content does not change, but the subject of the content is so mesmerizingly expansive, we are unable to process all there is to know about him.

Jesus' best friend, John, said it very accurately when he said, "Now there are also many other things that Jesus did. Were every one of them to be written, I suppose that the world itself could not contain the books that would be written" (John 21:25). John had seen Jesus do the miraculous time and time again. He even filled his Gospel with events that Matthew, Mark, and Luke neglected to report due to a simple judgment call of how much they could and should squeeze into their archival accounts. Out of all the incredible, mesmerizing, unthinkable acts that Jesus did, John is teaching that those four Gospels only scratched the surface. His proximity to Jesus for only three years could have filled more volumes of literature than could fit in the known world. The content of theology far surpasses the parameters of geography. We have more content on him than there is space to store it! If that is only three years worth of material, imagine how much more there is to report on God's eternal identity and activity?

While we are unable to search the depths of the knowledge of God thoroughly (Rom. 11:33-36) or grasp the wisdom of God fully (1 Cor. 2:7-9), God is the unrivaled expert on himself (1 Cor. 2:10-11). We don't know all there is to know about ourselves, and our material is limited and accessible. With God, infinite directions are spanning endless lengths, and yet he knows it all. While our grandest attempts at knowledge are still in the dark, "God is light and in him is no darkness at all" (1 John 1:5). He clearly sees how to navigate through all our theological crises by which we stumble in the shadows. The broad concepts and apparent tensions that leave us staggering are unable to faze him in the least. The more that we learn about God and find ourselves amazed, we realize that these are the mere fringes of his ways (Job 26:14). God has complete mastery over the most profound subject in the universe – himself.

Second, God has complete knowledge of the universe. As Creator, he fully comprehends his creation. "Great is our Lord, and abundant in power; his understanding is beyond measure" (Ps. 147:5). There is no subject beyond the expertise of God as his understanding is infinite.

He is perfect in knowledge. As humans, we are finite creatures attempting to comprehend the ways and the works of an infinite God. "Do you know the balancing of the clouds, the wondrous works of him who is perfect in knowledge" (Job 37:16). He is more than an expert; he is perfect in knowledge. He doesn't have a photographic memory that is comparatively impressive yet limited in scope. He knows absolutely everything (1 John 3:20).

Third, God has complete knowledge regarding the future. No potential or promised event in the future is blocked from the clear vision of God. He can see the future perfectly. "Remember the former things of old; for I am God, and there is no other; I am God, and there is none like me, declaring the end from the beginning and from ancient times things not yet done" (Isa. 46:9-10). As firmly as the past is solidified, the future is just as precisely sure to God. He actually declares the end before it has even started. From ancient times, he knew clearly what would happen in the future.

God can also see possible events clearly even if they will not come to pass. As David sought refuge from King Saul's murderous threats, he inquired of the LORD regarding his surrounding neighbors. He was unsure if the men of Keilah would be faithful to him or surrender him over to the ravenous Saul. The LORD replied, "They will surrender you" (1 Sam. 23:12). Thereafter, David departed from that region because of God's foreknowledge of something that never even came to pass (1 Sam. 23:13). God had complete knowledge of a scenario that never even actualized.

Jesus proved the point as he rebuked his shifty generation. Certain contemporaries of Jesus criticized him for his apparent loose living and rejected John the Baptist for his blatant strict guidelines (Matt. 11:18-19). They chastised both extremes. As Jesus exhorted his listeners, he cried out, "Woe to you, Chorazin! Woe to you, Bethsaida! For if the mighty works done in you had been done in Tyre and Sidon, they would have repented long ago in sackcloth and ashes" (Matt. 11:21). Jesus could look at an ancient city destroyed for their idolatry and see another possible future clearly if they had been privy to see his work. Unlike anyone else, God has complete knowledge regarding impending and potential future scenarios.

Finally, God has complete knowledge regarding us. "For he looks to the ends of the earth and sees everything under the heavens" (Job 28:24). We will not find an end of the world to which we can escape. God can always see us plainly and know us personally. There is not a detail of my life of which God does not know intimately. "No creature is hidden from his sight, but all are naked and exposed to the eyes of him to whom we must give account" (Heb. 4:13). God sees every skeleton in our closet as if it was a living and breathing reality. In our attempts to hide our messes from him, we are only creating deeper unnecessary issues for ourselves. If we would invest the time in addressing our problems rather than burying our messes, we could save ourselves from great heartache and headache.

God has every hair on my head (or the lack thereof) numbered (Matt. 10:30). While he knows precise details, he also knows spiritual realities. His eyes "run to and fro throughout the whole earth, to give strong support to those whose heart is blameless toward him" (2 Chr. 16:9). He sees straight through our manufactured religiosity and knows whether we are indeed his or not. God knew us even when we did not know him (Isa. 45:4). Every one of our days was seen as reality yet before we lived them (Ps. 139:16).

THE KNOWLEDGE WE NEED

If God does know everything, what does that mean for us? If all we know is that God knows everything, we will fair better than someone who thinks he or she knows it all on one's own. God's omniscience is the real science that we need.

This type of faith in God's omniscience doesn't provide a free pass to indulge in ignorance. On the contrary, it should drive us to seek all there is to know while maintaining a humble disposition that we will not be able to understand all there is to know until we intersect with eternity (Eccl. 3:11). We are to love the Lord our God with all of our minds (Mark 12:30) as well as our hearts, souls, and strength. As we fight against being conformed to this world, we should seek to be transformed by the renewal of our minds (Rom. 12:2). Such knowledge helps us prove what God's will is. As believers, we understand that it is an excellent thing to "grow in the grace and knowledge of our Lord and Savior Jesus Christ" (2 Pet. 3:18). The more that we know about God, the more that we will love about him. Every truth that he reveals grants us all the more reason to adore him. For every shred of knowledge we understand about God, we discover all the more reason to obsess over him with the entirety of our lives.

While we seek to increase our understanding, we must rest in our inability to be God. There is only one God, and you and I are not him. In relaying this information to you, I am not the bearer of bad news. A realization of who you are and who you are not is not a tragic development. Don't allow that fact to discourage you and bemoan your ignorance but rather encourage you to embrace his omniscience.

You don't have to know everything because God already does.

Rest in that reality! God is the supreme know-it-all, and he has never once been annoying about that fact. As an individual, it is a natural desire to possess all knowledge, but we are unable to handle such complexities. Our inability to procure omniscience should cause us to depend upon the only one who has it readily available.

God's Word is promised to be a lamp to our feet and a light to our path (Ps. 119:105) but not a layout to our future. Just like navigating yourself on a dark and dangerous terrain, your flashlight keeps you on the safest path. It doesn't provide enough light to cascade upon the distant destination, but it does illuminate that path enough to determine the next step. God's Word is like the flashlight intentionally keeping you dependent upon his knowledge for every step of the journey and graciously disallowing you to see the entire path in one glance.

Why would he not just give us insight into the whole picture now? Shouldn't God just share with us this valuable knowledge? If God showed me the entire path clearly, I would cease to seek him diligently. The pursuit is part of the journey. If we possessed the whole map, we would express gratitude to him for the information and yet move on our way to fulfill his plan while neglecting him in the process. Thank God that he doesn't share all of his knowledge with us.

Not only does God's complete knowledge help us reorient ourselves to him, but it also alleviates unnecessary responsibility on our part. God isn't dependent upon your credentials or notifications. You will never inform God of anything. We often pray as if we are God's briefing team. As we fire off our list, we desperately seek to find the last name of the person we are talking about to help make sure he doesn't mix him up with another. Our requests sound like we are letting him in on a secret to which he was not previously aware. We confess our thoughts and actions as if they were breaking news to him.

God knows everything. He even knows the stuff you are trying to keep under wraps. Stop trying to hide from him what he already sees clearly. I acknowledge that my brain never stops. Among the few noble thoughts I have during the day, I am also plagued with unsavory ideas running across my psyche. Ashamed, I waste time attempting to block God out from consciousness.

Paul taught that we should take "every thought captive to obey Christ" (2 Cor. 10:5). If I'm aware my sinful thoughts exist, Jesus is also aware that those sinful thoughts exist, and when I become aware that he is aware, I'm on the path to victory. He already knows where we are struggling. Stop pridefully acting like you can set up a forcefield to block him from your thoughts. Acknowledge the Omnipotent God who is eager to join you in the fight. He knows it all. God is aware of where you struggle, and he can point you to the path of success. Take advantage of that. You don't need to envy possession of what God promises to provide. Depend upon him for his knowledge.

✂ OMNISCIENCE REVIEW

Incorrect Perception: ~~God is an undergraduate~~.

Correct Attribute: *God is omniscient.*

Definition: *The omniscience of God means that he is all-knowing.*

Focal Verse: *Great is our Lord, and abundant in power; his understanding is beyond measure (Ps. 147:5).*

Implication: *You don't have to know everything because God already does.*

🗔 FURTHER STUDY

What specific thought from this chapter challenged your thinking?

Meditate on Job 38:1-18. As you read, realize that God is finally speaking to Job regarding his questions. Responding to Job's questions, what does God's response teach us about himself?

When comparing God's knowledge to ours, how should that affect the way we approach him?

📋 CORRECTIVE THEOLOGY

What do you honestly wish you knew of which you are currently ignorant?

How does God denying us the power of omniscience cause us to address him?

What is it that God knows right now that provides you comfort?

CHAPTER 10
THE POLLSTER GOD

A pollster in our culture is someone who organizes, conducts, and analyzes opinion polls. Due to their research, they can take a cross-section of society, ask some pertinent questions, and provide the rest of the culture with information regarding the leanings of the majority of people polled. In light of this information, many people will acknowledge the trends, adjust their thinking, and align their methods with popular opinion. Whether it is the type of presidential candidate the people are looking for or the kind of menu the restaurant should be offering, we are prone to gather opinions from the masses to determine the direction for our organizations.

If you haven't noticed, the culture is rapidly changing. That's why the Pollster God is such an alluring candidate for our societal flavor-of-the-month theology. Because we can't fathom adhering to archaic directives in such a progressive time, the Pollster God exists to ascertain what people want and then give it to them. As soon as he obtains the direction of the culture, he adjusts his thinking to be relevant with the times. If the prevailing attitude of the society has a particular bent, we assume that God will align himself with the majority's leanings. What's ironic about this line of thinking is that each culture is consistently rebuking the culture before it because of its defective perspectives and dangerous practices. The beliefs that a current culture criticizes were usually embraced by the majority of the culture previously. So why do we think that our current trends will fair any differently when judged by history? This might come as a startling offense to the cultural masses, but God is not tracking with our bizarre directions to determine a new line of thinking or an altered course of action.

God is not a pollster. God is supremely wise.

THE WISDOM OF GOD

Studying the attributes of God, it is critical to address the issue of God's wisdom. Can God be trusted to make the right decisions? Are God's thoughts always the best thoughts? Does he need to align himself with us or do we need to align ourselves with him? God's wisdom is different than his omniscience. God's omniscience teaches that he knows all things; God's wisdom teaches that he knows all the wise things to do.

As believers, it is growing increasingly difficult to defend the wisdom of God through our beliefs and display the wisdom of God through our behaviors. To follow the wisdom of God means that you will be swimming against society's current. In our culture, even churches feel the growing temptation to listen to the popular leanings of the day to determine their positions and adapt their practices regarding current issues. The wisdom of God balks at any stance limited by time and culture. If a concept only has a temporal shelf life, it cannot be categorized as truth. Only God can determine, define, and demand enduring wisdom.

The wisdom of God means that only God knows how to come to the best destination by the best path at the best time. When we speak of a wise person, we often envision a senior sage able to provide thorough and balanced counsel to others in unsure situations. While we attribute some of the person's intellect as coming from books and lectures, we usually hold that wisdom comes more from age and experience. The wise examples in our lives are often those who have received honorary doctorates from the school of hard knocks. Their quality of life in the later stages teaches us that their insights are trustworthy.

Since we call others wise, it seems a tad too simple to categorize God into the same assemblage. His infinite wisdom compared to our limited intelligence is more than the separation of advanced calculus to simple arithmetic. His wisdom infinitely transcends the very concept of knowledge. God is not merely wise; he is supremely wise. He is unable to make the imperfect call. God's decisions have never been unwise. To God alone belong wisdom and might (Dan. 2:20). Therefore, if any person can claim any level of keen sense, it must originate from God. Every wise person must discover their bearings by the totality of God's wisdom.

God's wisdom is unlimited in its scope. The wisest human beings can master specific disciplines, yet they each experience some degree of limitation. God has no constraint on the amount or the category of his wisdom. You wouldn't give a pastor with a doctorate in theology the permission to perform open-heart surgery. While the degree is impressive, it does not apply to the situation at hand.

God will never find a discipline in which he is not the wisest expert there is.

God's wisdom over creation justifies his wisdom for creation. In God's unique wisdom, he founded the world (Prov. 3:19) and was able to create and sustain all good works that we can behold (Ps. 104:24). He "established the world by his wisdom, and by his understanding stretched out the heavens" (Jer. 10:12). If God is every creature's beginning, it implies that he is also their end. The only wise God able to create all things is the only one wise enough to teach wisdom sufficient for creation. God is wise in heart, and our attempts to harden ourselves against him are futile (Job 9:4).

God's wisdom can never be slightly improved. If God's plans could become wiser by any iota, that implies that they are initially imperfect which would mean he would not be God. For us, hindsight is 20/20, but for God, foresight is 20/20. He has never looked back in the rearview mirror wishing he would have spoken or acted differently. His wisdom guarantees that even his timing and manner are ever impeccable. His understanding is infinite and without limitations. "Great is our Lord, and abundant in power; his understanding is beyond measure" (Ps. 147:5). If God isn't wise, we are in trouble. We require authority over us. Praise be to God that this supreme authority is supremely wise!

God's wisdom doesn't require input from others. His sense is brilliantly flawless and unequivocally independent of any outside help – he is only wise (Rom. 16:27). The depth of his understanding is inscrutable (Rom. 11:33). God is not dependent upon the assistance of angels, the suggestions of followers, or the opinions of the masses to decide his direction. Each of us has reached those crossroads where we desperately needed a listening ear or an outside estimation to help us discern a situation. Unable to make the call, we depended upon supposedly unbiased help to chart the course. While some of those decisions were healthy, we still flubbed many of the resolutions for which we received counsel. God has informed others regarding his decisions, but he has never relied on others to determine his decisions. His leading has always been unceasingly wise.

God's wisdom must always be viewed in light of eternity. Immediate reactions and responses can never grapple with the weight of eternal wisdom. Craftiness can choose the most favorable option at the moment, but only understanding can determine the most glorifying decision for eternity. If you are questioning God's wisdom in a moment, have you stepped back to remember that this moment, while maybe feeling like an eternity, is actually leading us to eternity? We question the wisdom of God when we focus on the current situation rather than the future glory (Rom. 8:18). It takes time for true wisdom to be vindicated. God's brilliance regarding his wisdom might be incomprehensible until future generations confirm it (Luke 7:35). Even his ability to assemble such a unique, multicultural people over history displays the unmatched, manifold wisdom of God (Eph. 3:10).

God's wisdom is available yet restricted. "His divine power has granted to us all things that pertain to life and godliness, through the knowledge of him who called us to his own glory and excellence" (2 Pet. 1:3). Every bit of wisdom that we need has been provided, but not every bit of wisdom that we desire has been made available. Just like in Eden, there are some pieces of God's knowledge that we are not yet to know (Gen. 2:17). The fear of the LORD is the beginning of wisdom (Prov. 1:7; 9:10), but there is some wisdom that God does not provide with us currently. He makes everything beautiful in its time by placing "eternity into man's heart, yet so that he cannot find out what God has done from the beginning to the end" (Ecc. 3:11). God has placed a longing for eternity in our hearts but lacking a complete understanding of it. We cannot yet handle the secret things that belong to the LORD our God (Deut. 29:29). While we cannot ascertain all of his reasonings right now or why he allows what he allows (2 Cor. 12:7-10), we can trust that he is working all things together for the good of those who love him and are called according to his purpose (Rom. 8:28). Even that acceptance is a submission to the glorious wisdom and timing of God. You cannot rush the timing of history's affirmation of his wisdom. God's ways will ultimately be confirmed, but they were never promised to be popular. This wisdom, though it often seems secret and hidden, will endure throughout eternity (1 Cor. 2:7).

God's wisdom rarely provides instant gratification. In God's presence, there is the fullness of joy, and at his right hand, there are pleasures forevermore (Ps. 16:11). While God does give great blessings to us now, there are also some that are held back until we are finally in his presence. Will we be willing to forsake the scraps of this world to feast at the table of heaven? The wisdom of the world seeks to provide immediate pleasure (Prov. 9:17) while the wisdom of the Word can provide lasting joy (Prov. 9:6). The wisdom of God guides us to make decisions for our eternal joy rather than our temporal happiness. Jesus said that it was better to sever a body part in this life than to forgo the glories of heaven (Matt. 18:7-9). No one desiring instant gratification would ever agree to such an aggressive tactic to fight temptation. Only those who, like Moses, know that it is better to "be mistreated with the people of God than to enjoy the fleeting pleasures of sin. He considered the reproach of Christ greater wealth than the treasures of Egypt, for he was looking to the reward" (Heb. 11:25-26). You can offer a definitive "no" now for a glorious "yes" later.

God's wisdom should alter our daily decisions. His counsel is more than a lofty collection of theological pontifications. He expects us to live out his principles in our lives. While God's wisdom is applicable in every situation imaginable throughout every day of history, what personal benefit is it to you if you fail to apply it? The infinite wisdom of God is meant to be transferred to our finite decisions today. The Holy Spirit can teach us all understanding and bring to our minds the truths that we have forgotten (John 14:26). He is able and willing to recall that information for us in the needed hour.

If we lack wisdom, God has promised to give it to us if we only ask in faith (Jas. 1:5-6). Are you desirous of God's will? What a relieving notion to know that God wants you in his will even more than you want it. As he renews our minds, we are positioned to discern "the will of God, what is good and acceptable and perfect" (Rom. 12:2). As we acknowledge him in all of our ways, he can make our paths straight (Prov. 3:6).

God is the source of wisdom equipping us with his counsel and understanding to make sound decisions in this life (Job 12:13). King Solomon wisely asked for wisdom when given the opportunity to ask God for any type of help (1 Kgs. 3:9). God is the originator and deliverer of correct understanding (Prov. 2:6). If we obtain God's wisdom, every right perspective falls into place. God delights in his truth dwelling in us, and he teaches us wisdom in our hearts (Ps. 51:6). No one obtains sense unless God gives it to him or her (Dan. 2:21). God has promised that he "will lead the blind in a way that they do not know, in paths that they have not known" (Isa. 42:16).

THE DISCERNMENT WE NEED

God's wisdom provides the needed discernment for our lives. He is supremely and unapologetically wise. We are not. His instructions for our lives are for our benefit, and yet we suspect him to have sinisterly ulterior motives. While the purpose for obeying his commands finds its root in God's glory, its fruit is for our good. No one has ever regretted following God's wisdom, yet we all know the painful realization that our chance at peace went missing in those moments when we relentlessly committed to disobedience (Isa. 48:18).

Will we rely on him? As his wise instructions come to us, we have three ways to respond. Regarding God's wisdom, each of us is either ignorant, stubborn, or wise. Which one are you currently?

If you are ignorant, that means that you aren't aware of his wisdom. For those who have never actually investigated the claims of Scripture, you may honestly be ignorant concerning what the wisdom of God is. You might be more abreast with the trends of the culture than the truths of the Bible. Let me assure you: God's wisdom is not a cosmic killjoy but a serious merrymaker. As you seek out the understanding of God heralded through the Scriptures, you will find the most reasonable and delightful insights for life. Do your personal best to study the Word so you can present yourself to God unashamed as you accurately handle his words of truth (2 Tim. 2:15). His Word makes the simple wise (Ps. 19:7). If applied, his wisdom makes you unique among all other people (Deut. 4:6-8).

If you are stubborn, that means that you recognize his wisdom but are unwilling to heed it. The difference between the ignorant and the stubborn is awareness. While ignorant people have some margin of excuse, stubborn individuals have none. You know precisely what God's Word says regarding the wisest way to live, and you rebel against it defiantly. God says right, and you are determined to go left. With a tiny clenched fist raised up towards the massive skies, you think your way is better than his. You need to repent, and you need to repent now. Every stubborn defiance is robbing you of living in the center of God's superior wisdom.

If you are wise, that means that you are aware of God's wisdom and seeking to be obedient. You comprehend that fearing the LORD is the starting place for knowledge, and if applied, you exhibit good understanding (Ps. 111:10). This type of biblical wisdom should never puff up the recipient but rather humble the benefactor (Prov. 11:2; Jas. 3:13). We should be gleefully grateful that the Spirit of God desires to pass his wisdom to us (Isa. 11:2; John 14:26), and embolden us to apply it (Phil. 2:13; Col. 1:29). To obey this wisdom, we must walk according to the Spirit and not according to the flesh (Rom. 8:4).

We all have received God's wisdom yet rejected it. God's wisdom descended at Mt. Sinai, and our disobedience to it led him to ascend upon Mt. Calvary. The provision of God's wisdom came through the commandments, and the protection against its consequences went through the cross. Since none of us can keep it perfectly, God, in his understanding, sent Jesus to rescue us from our foolish ways of living. Jesus on the cross displays the grand wisdom of God (1 Cor. 1:24). The stability of this life and the security of the next life comes down to whose wisdom you prioritize. Choose wisely.

✂ **WISDOM** REVIEW

Incorrect Perception: ~~God is a pollster~~.

Correct Attribute: *God is supremely wise.*

Definition: *The wisdom of God means that only he knows how to come to the best destination by the best path at the best time.*

Focal Verse: *Oh, the depth of the riches and wisdom and knowledge of God! How unsearchable are his judgments and how inscrutable his ways (Rom. 11:33)!*

Implication: *God's wisdom provides the needed discernment for our lives.*

🗐 **FURTHER** STUDY

What specific thought from this chapter deepened your devotion?

Meditate on Proverbs 9:7-12. What traits are evident within a person who listens to the wisdom of God?

How is fearing the LORD (Prov. 9:10) practically seen as the beginning of wisdom?

📋 **CORRECTIVE** THEOLOGY

Logically, how can any current cultural leaning not equate with the wisdom of God?

Regarding God's wisdom, would you currently refer yourself to being ignorant, stubborn, or wise? Why?

What piece of God's wisdom are you desperately seeking to know?

CHAPTER 11
THE PERMISSION-SEEKING GOD

At every stage of life, we each know the annoying nature of having to ask permission from a higher authority. As a child, we longed for the days when we could eat as many cookies whenever we wanted, ignite fireworks in the most confined of places, and entertain ourselves with whatever mediums that suited our fancy. Those pesky parents were regularly serving as annoying guardrails as they reminded us they could care less about what Johnny's parents let him do because they weren't Johnny's parents. We dreamt of a day in which we would no longer have to succumb to needing anyone's permission. As we grew older, we realized that requiring a permit to meet our desires never went away. The teachers threatened detention, the police officers decelerated our pace, the government indulged upon our paychecks, and the boss expected punctuality. Even as we progressed through life, we realized that someone is always keeping us in check at every level. The boss always has a boss. Even if it is a board of trustees holding a long leash, at some point, every head honcho can be called into question by some governing authority. The president himself can even be vetoed by a conglomeration of senators whom he bested in the primaries and general election. If the president himself can be called into question, who is immune from such scrutiny?

For many of us, we don't even think God is immune. When you listen to us speak of God, we often characterize him as needing our permission. When confronted with a situation that we dislike, we either question the will of God or use the devil as a scapegoat. When facing a moral crisis in our culture, we blame the lack of voter turnout for the current direction of an administration. When our theological biases are challenged, we avoid certain verses of Scripture and base our positions on our feelings. God couldn't be like "that." Why? Because a God like that doesn't meet our expectations. We speak as if God is awaiting our approval. In essence, our resentful opposition to his methods indicates that we believe we deserve the right to make the call more than God does. Our displeasure in his actions makes a passive-aggressive case for our own sovereignty over the Sovereign God.

God is not seeking our permission. God is sovereign.

THE SOVEREIGNTY OF GOD

Out of all the attributes, I do not believe one is as hotly-contested as God's sovereignty. We were taught as children that the whole world is in God's hands, and we each believe that to some extent. How he exerts his control is what divides the Church into some of the most warring factions present throughout religious history. Believers all hold that God is in control but by how much?

The sovereignty of God means that God has the sole authority to have complete control over the universe. Jesus possesses all power in heaven and on earth (Matt. 28:18), and no one on earth has access to a fraction of it unless God wills it (Rom. 13:1). He is utterly unique in his claim to authority. He has asked permission from no one, and no one can strip him of it. That authority provides him complete control over all creation. If there is anything that is beyond his control, that will prove he is not God. The entity able to escape the grasp of this God would actually steal the title away with such a blatant usurpation.

While he has the authority to do all things, that does not imply that he does all things. Could God play the puppeteer and make us each dance upon his stage in the way he sees fit? Yes, he *can*. God has the authority to do whatever he wills. Does he? Not always.

Nearing the cross, Jesus looked over Jerusalem and cried, "How often would I have gathered your children together as a hen gathers her brood under her wings, and you were not willing!" (Matt. 22:37). Does this verse imply that Jesus wanted something but couldn't find a way to do it? Not a chance. When the ruler Herod was looking to kill Jesus, he replied, "Go tell that fox, 'Look, I will keep driving out demons and healing people today and tomorrow, and on the third day I will reach my goal'" (Luke 13:32). The most powerful authority in the region sought Jesus out, and Jesus refused him an appointment until it was convenient on his schedule. He told them to inform Herod he was busy at the moment, and he would be there to die when he was good and ready! That type of authority could have gathered the city together if he wanted. The Sovereign God could have pulled the puppet strings or wired the robotic circuits to huddle them together immediately, but he didn't. They were unwilling, and he let it be.

The tension of God's sovereignty against man's free will is the paramount issue regarding this attribute. If God is truly sovereign, is anything outside of his control? Does anyone have any authority to make even the simplest of decisions? While these allotted pages will never suffice to answer a question that has been plaguing theologians for centuries, we still must wrestle with this concept if we are to obtain a thoroughly biblical theology.

God is sovereign, and man is responsible. While this paradigm seems contradictory, they are actually complementary. If we are given such rights to make individual decisions, God must maintain control or else chaos would reign. While we may want him to have limited power, he can have nothing of the sort. God is wholly sovereign, or he is not sovereign at all. Our tensions reveal that we desire God to be in absolute control as long as we still maintain the power to veto his decisions when we deem necessary. We unjustifiably hold that he should seek our endorsement for actions that directly affect us. If God has to seek our permission, that implies we are sovereign and not him.

Are we truly free to make our own decisions? It depends. I am free to choose between chocolate or vanilla. I have the opportunity to marry this woman or that woman. I can make the call to give or to take. God freely gives me such freedom. God's authority even grants me a certain level of authority. "See, I have set before you today life and good, death and evil" (Deut. 30:15).

We do have a considerable amount of freedom, but we are also restricted significantly. I am unable to give myself wings to fly. I do not possess the power to change my ethnicity. I am not able to change the path of admission into heaven. Why? Because God is sovereign and I am not. "Our God is in the heavens; he does all that he pleases" (Ps. 115:3). In this complexity, we discover frustration yet brilliance. In his sovereignty, God has complete control to allow us limited control. The tension and yet the resolution is seen succinctly in the decision of Judas' betrayal. Jesus came to Earth on a mission for the cross (John 12:27), and yet Judas' deceitful treason was the catalyst for Jesus' arrest. "For the Son of Man goes as it is written of him, but woe to that man by whom the Son of Man is betrayed!" (Mark 14:21).

Was God sovereign or Judas responsible? Yes. While it appears as if there is tension, there can be none. Jesus' divine sovereignty over the cross never negated Judas' human responsibility of his betrayal. It must stay in this tension because the two other options are unthinkable. If God was surprised by Judas' betrayal, that means he is not sovereign, and the future is unknown. If God is the catalyst behind sinful choices, that means we are not responsible, and God ordains sin. Judas made his choice under the jurisdiction of the unshakeable sovereignty of God. As evidenced in this uniquely pivotal moment of redemptive history, God can even use the sinful actions of men to accomplish his grand purposes. The sovereignty of God confirms that he can bring all things together for good to those who love him and are called according to his purpose (Rom. 8:28). We do not need to seek reconciliation between God's sovereignty and man's responsibility because they have never been at odds with one another.

THE AUTHORITY WE NEED

As we attempt to grasp the sovereignty of God, it renders some people immobile because they wrongly assume that their decisions now mean nothing. Why evangelize if God is sovereign over salvation? Why plead with this person to change a way of life if God determines if a person gets it or not? Why worry about sinful leanings since God can even use our evil choices? On the contrary, we should relish the opportunity to choose well according to the limited options we have been given. In the sovereignty of God, he has sovereignly purposed that prayer makes a difference, the gospel is the power to salvation, a loving intentionality can save a home, and the preparation in the Word equips you for moments of which you are unaware. He is sovereignly working through the opportunities he gives us.

Not only does God sovereignly decide the end, but he also sovereignly determines the means.

God's sovereignty guarantees that his agenda will go through regardless of our decisions. You and I can get it together and join his cause or be left in the dust. His plan isn't dependent upon a revolutionary band of willing participants. He is not antsy about the outcome. God is entirely sovereign over creation. He rules over all (1 Chr. 29:11), and no purpose of his can be thwarted (Job 42:2). "The LORD has established his throne in the heavens, and his kingdom rules over all" (Ps. 103:19). The LORD does whatever he pleases in heaven and on earth (Ps. 135:6). God is the one who holds our very breath (Dan. 5:23), and you can guarantee that not a single inhale or exhale takes place without his provision. Within his sovereign control, he has granted us certain freedoms in accordance with his plan.

God is uniquely sovereign over history. While the constant ebb and flow of mankind's advances and setbacks never cease to baffle us, God maintains the charted course without once being surprised at the developments. "All the inhabitants of the earth are accounted as nothing, and he does according to his will among the host of heaven and among the inhabitants of the earth; and none can stay his hand or say to him, 'What have you done?'" (Dan. 4:35). God can turn even the king's heart whichever way he so desires (Prov. 21:1). God's throne trumps every other throne as he positions all into and removes all from authority (Rom. 13:1). It is essential for us all to know "that the Most High rules the kingdom of men and gives it to whom he will and sets over it the lowliest of men" (Dan. 4:17).

God is sovereign over suffering. While it may be uncomfortable to admit, God allows suffering but also personally initiates it at times. "I form light and create darkness, I make well-being and create calamity, I am the LORD, who does all these things" (Isa. 45:7). God is the one who wounds and heals (Deut. 32:39). Realize that Jesus on the cross was the most undeservingly gruesome case of suffering in all of history, and yet it provided an eternity of heavenly joy for the redeemed. God can sovereignly use temporal moments of unjust suffering for eternal realities of unthinkable grace.

God is sovereign over salvation. While warring camps will continue their debates over this issue until Jesus clarifies it to us all in glory, we must commit to what Scripture teaches. I believe God would be more honored and souls would be more prepared if we would spend more time sharing with others about salvation than we do debating with each other about salvation.

God alone has the authoritative right to predestination (Eph. 1:11). Jesus even stated, "No one can come to me unless the Father who sent me draws him" (John 6:44). God has "mercy on whomever he wills, and he hardens whomever he wills" (Rom. 9:18). In Romans 9, Paul defends difficult doctrines. He highlights the supreme right that God has to do whatever he wants to do. He chose Jacob over Esau because that was his desire (Rom. 9:11). God further hardened Pharaoh's stony heart so that God's power over him would be proclaimed in all the earth (Rom. 9:17).

While such practices may seem unsettling to us, God has a prepared response: "Who are you, O man, to answer back to God? Will what is molded say to its molder, 'Why have you made me like this?'" (Rom. 9:20). How can the simple challenge the Sovereign? Whatever God says about salvation is his prerogative. Do you think your thorough argument should warrant a change of policy on his behalf? He is God. He can do whatever he wants to do! That's the point of this passage. He highlights specific events and declares the right to do it. Does he say in this passage that he hardens every other heart? No. His authority is defended more than his activity is defined. Biblical scholars will warn readers from using descriptive portions of Scripture as prescriptive doctrinal stances. This passage does teach that God is sovereign over salvation, and yet the following chapter explains the importance for us sharing the gospel for salvation.

"For everyone who calls on the name of the Lord will be saved" (Rom. 10:13). In Romans 9, God seems to choose those for salvation, and in Romans 10, God seems to provide access to anyone who calls on him for salvation. Which one is it? It is both. Calvinists' favorite chapter of the Bible is Romans 9, and Arminianists' is Romans 10. We would be wise to realize that these two are next door neighbors and get along just fine. Even while you may drift towards one camp or another, show godly charity towards brother and sisters in Christ. A biblical belief should produce a humble disposition.

It is difficult for finite minds to reconcile but not for an infinite God to provide. Just as Jesus reminded that one sparrow doesn't fall to the ground without God's involvement (Matt. 10:29), he reaffirms the potential for whosoever to come to him moments later (Matt. 10:32-33). Scripture affirms God's sovereignty and man's responsibility. God has placed eternity in our hearts where we cannot understand it completely (Ecc. 3:11). No matter how many theological degrees you possess, there are some secret things you simply don't know (Deut. 29:29). I would propose a fundamental unifying question for us all to consider: who is the initiator and provider of salvation? Since Jesus is the author and perfecter of our faith (Heb. 12:2), we should never seek to take credit for salvation. We should all agree that Jesus is ultimately responsible. All we did was provide the need for salvation!

God is also sovereign over his agenda. He is the initiator of salvation through the free opportunities of sharing the gospel with others. He is moving us to his redemptive climax sovereignly determined before the foundation of the world (Eph. 1:4; Rom. 8:29; Rev. 13:8). The LORD even has a purpose for the wicked (Prov. 16:4). What we see coming to pass is because the Lord has commanded it to be (Lam. 3:37). Does God interfere? Sure he does. Just like a father sees his toddler child conspiring for disobedience, that father can stop that child whenever he wants. Sometimes he does, and sometimes he allows that child to disobey and suffer the consequences. The father was still in authority by allowing a certain level of control to the child. God is sovereign. He is free even in our freedom. He is in control even despite our limited control. Praise be to him who has never sought our permission! Could you imagine what this world would be like if the outcomes were contingent upon our approval?

✂ SOVEREIGNTY REVIEW

Incorrect Perception: ~~God is seeking our permission~~.

Correct Attribute: *God is sovereign.*

Definition: *The sovereignty of God means that God has the sole authority to have complete control over the universe.*

Focal Verse: *Our God is in the heavens; he does all that he pleases (Ps. 115:3).*

Implication: *We never have to fear that any situation is out of control because God is ultimately sovereign.*

🗐 FURTHER STUDY

What particular idea from this chapter challenged you?

Meditate on Daniel 4:28-37. Why was it necessary for God to prove his sovereignty to King Nebuchadnezzar?

How does Daniel 4:35 conflict with many modern ideas about our abilities and God's sovereignty?

CORRECTIVE THEOLOGY

What are your personal pushbacks to the idea that God is entirely sovereign?

What would be the dangers if God wasn't in full control?

To fear God's control reveals we fear his heart. What about God's performance should cause you to distrust his lone authority?

CHAPTER 12
THE UNRELIABLE GOD

Many people follow the Unreliable God – that is if they can somehow discover an adequate way to track him. His ideas are too uncertain, and his methods are too shifty. The task of figuring out where he is and what he is doing is a daunting challenge. And when and if you actually do find him, you never know what type of mood he will be in once you see him.

The Unreliable God is walking around with some significant baggage left by numerous people in our lives. Each of us knows what it feels like to be forgotten and isolated. Too many people have broken some precious promises which led us to some serious consequences. Each time that someone failed to keep his or her word, we built emotional walls up higher than we ever thought possible. To keep ourselves safe, we learned to keep people out.

Your dad was never around. Your mom was too busy. Your significant other moved you to an insignificant standing. The company closed. The mentor fell. Your letdowns became almost too expected and normative. You began to think that the only sure thing in this life was that people disappoint you.

Imagine a boy sitting on a bench beside a field. As he repeatedly tosses the baseball into his glove, he continually scans the area looking for the promise maker. Even though something came up last week, his hero promised that they would play ball together today. Minutes go by, and he realizes that his mentor isn't just a few seconds behind. His gleeful anticipation is eventually replaced with despairing rejection.

Once again, he got his hopes up for nothing. Why on earth did he ever imagine that today would be different than any other day? He finally began to accept the painful reality that those who we look up to have an incredible capacity for letting us down.

Along the way, we make God pay for the mistakes of others. For all the people who have proven to be unreliable, we associate their nature with God's character. We stare at the promises of God and demand that we receive a deadline of when they will come to pass. We confuse God's reliability with our expectations of how and when he should do it. When God doesn't do things the way we want it, and when we want it, we decry his methods and question his motives. Since God doesn't operate according to our preferences, we claim him to be unreliable.

God is not unreliable. God is faithful.

THE FAITHFULNESS OF GOD

Unlike the god of our making, the God of the Bible epitomizes faithfulness. While people are characterized by unfaithful transgressions and faithless decisions, God reassures his faithfulness time and time again. In fact, all of the other attributes are uniquely dependent upon this one. If God's holiness is not faithful, he will periodically change his stance on issues of morality. If God's mercy is not constant, he will second guess his decisions and change his mind when he is having a bad day. If God's omnipotence is not reliable, he will encounter certain obstacles of which he is helpless. The attribute of God's faithfulness ensures that all of the other attributes remain consistent.

The faithfulness of God means that whatever God says is entirely true and it will truly come to pass. In a world characterized by lies and deceit, what glorious truth to behold – there is one who speaks the full truth all the time! This attribute enlightens the mind but should also invigorate the heart. Our God is faithful in his faithfulness. God's faithfulness displays itself in four critical areas. God is faithful because his words are true, his promises are reliable, his assistance is available, and his character is consistent.

12: THE UNRELIABLE GOD

First, God is trustworthy. We can know without the shadow of a doubt that all of his words are true. As people, we are commanded not to lie (Exod. 20:16), but a hallmark of our identity is that we are liars (Num. 23:19). We are called not to lie to one another (Col. 3:9), but our deceitful tongues plot inevitable destruction in our lives (Ps. 52:2), and they serve as an abomination to the LORD (Prov. 12:22). Just a sampling of our culture should enable us to echo the prophet Isaiah who said, "Woe is me! For I am lost; for I am a man of unclean lips, and I dwell in the midst of a people of unclean lips" (Isa. 6:5). In our sinful state, we identify more with the sneaky, serpentine Satan who is the father of lies (John 8:44) than our reliable, responsible Redeemer whose very name in heaven is Faithful and True (Rev. 19:11).

While lies depict our culture, God's faithfulness ensures that every single one of his words is trustworthy. In a world full of lies, God's words come from a different type of quality. God's faithfulness means that he has never lied in the past, and he will continue to be free from deceit in the future. If his words are trustworthy, we can presume that each promise of his will genuinely and eventually come to pass.

Second, God is reliable. We can take every promise of God all the way to the bank. For all the extensive lists of promises made by God in Scripture, every single one of them finds their "yes" and "amen" in Christ (2 Cor. 1:20). While we typically reserve the word, "amen," for the conclusion of a prayer, the word actually means, "it is true." Whenever Jesus would say, "truly, truly I say to you," he was saying, "amen, amen, I say to you." As we pray, especially in light of God's promises, our punctuation to our intercessions is a confident confession that what we just prayed is undeniably trustworthy. If God has promised it, you can rely on it with your entire being.

Whatever God has promised, he will do (Num. 23:19). God is not a wishy-washy deity with the possibility of changing his mind (1 Sam. 15:29). When he makes a covenant with his people, he will not violate it (Ps. 89:34) but remembers it forever (Ps. 105:8). God promised the unfaithful Jacob that he would continue his faithfulness to him and would not leave him until he had done what he had pledged to him (Gen. 28:15). Praise to this faithful God who has promised that he will finish what he started in us (Phil. 1:6)!

While many of us acknowledge that God's words are reliable, they are not often as expedient as we would prefer. Remember that God's ways are not our ways (Isa. 55:8). Realize that God's promises have an eternal shelf life. Even the hope of his return might feel like slowness to us given the current condition of this world, but do not mistake God's patience with your perspective of slowness (2 Pet. 3:9). His timing is not our timing. What seems like a day to us might be a thousand years to him, or what feels like a thousand years to us might be a day to him (2 Pet. 3:8). God's promises deserve a patient open door from us and not an impatient stopwatch. He does have good plans for our future (Jer. 29:11), but, like the Israelites, we might have to wait seventy years before they are realized (Jer. 29:10). Even while we wait, we can be strong and take courage because his promises are trustworthy (Ps. 27:14).

Third, God is willing. His assistance to address temptation is available. In the character and activity of God, we see a thorough willingness to come to our aid in temptation. God's words are valid. His promises are faithful. Sometimes, we just confuse what he actually said. Many people will say that "God will never put on you more than you can bear." I respectfully disagree. In fact, I think God has often put on me more than I can bear so that I will come to him with it.

The verse that this saying references (and partially quotes) is 1 Cor. 10:13 which reads, "No temptation has overtaken you that is not common to man. God is faithful, and he will not let you be tempted beyond your ability, but with the temptation he will also provide the way of escape, that you may be able to endure it." The verse has more to do with temptation than trials. God promised we would never be tempted beyond what we can bear.

How can we avoid irresistible temptation? God has promised us success during such moments. Is it because we are that faithful? Absolutely not! In this verse, the Apostle Paul appeals to God's faithfulness – not ours. If we can be faithful through temptation, it is because God is faithful to us. He has promised that every time temptation rears its ugly head, he will provide a prudent path of escape. Like a fire escape plan for a burning building, God has promised that every time the singes of temptation starts nearing your soul, he opens an escape hatch and points you towards safety. As we pray for him not to lead us into temptation (Matt. 6:13), we are assured that he will never tempt us (Jas. 1:13) and that he will always guide us to a safe path away from the temptation (1 Cor. 10:13).

Finally, God's faithfulness is displayed in one crucially additional arena. While God's words are true, his promises can be trusted, and his willingness to help us in temptation is guaranteed, he is also faithful in his consistent character. He is who he says he is, and no one can change him. You never have to worry about encountering an emotionally-laden, inconsistent God.

While sleep patterns, eating schedules, weather conditions, employment stress, and relational drama can each alter our dispositions critically, the totality of history's unfolding rebellion has yet to change who God is. Never once has jadedness robbed him of his character. Anger has never enraged him so that he stepped out of line from his previously ordained plan. God's consistent nature is the most reliable standard there is, and yet he has endured the most consistent and complete rebellion there is. Since Adam and Eve first gnawed on disobedience, God has withstood rebellious rejections, unthinkable uprisings, and downright debaucheries antithetical to his standards and character. Through all the insanity wrongfully wrought by humanity, God has faithfully remained who he has always been. Our unfaithfulness was unable to dilute God's faithfulness.

We are desperately in need of the faithfulness of God due to the unfaithfulness of us. Paul told Timothy, "If we are faithless, he remains faithful – for he cannot deny himself" (2 Tim. 2:13). His character will not allow unfaithfulness on his part! The attribute of God's faithfulness is paramount to our unfaithful survival.

Our great hope is in the consistent faithfulness of God. His wondrous steadfast nature causes our mouths to sing of his faithfulness and to declare it to all generations (Ps. 89:1). No matter which era you inhabit, God remains faithful throughout every age. As we gather with his people, we look upward to the heavens which scream his faithfulness (Ps. 89:5). His reliability encompasses every single one of his works. Faithfulness literally surrounds everything he does (Ps. 89:8). How could such a faithful God endure such unfaithful people? Because he provides us with his faithfulness and mercy (Ps. 89:24)!

Our part is to confess our unfaithful nature resulting in sin, and he promises to be faithful and just to forgive us our sins and even to cleanse us from all of our unrighteousness (1 John 1:9). How can we be guaranteed of such incredible promises? "He who calls you is faithful; he will surely do it" (1 Thess. 5:24). Because we are faithless, we need the type of mercy that can only be found in the faithfulness of the LORD. "The steadfast love of the LORD never ceases; his mercies never come to an end; they are new every morning; great is your faithfulness" (Lam. 3:22-23).

THE RELIABILITY WE NEED

God is perfectly reliable, yet we live as if we are unsure if he will come through when we need him most. The greatest challenge to us embracing God's faithfulness is our own forgetfulness. Many believers theologically hold to the attribute of God's faithfulness but practically deny it with their lives. Allow a new challenging circumstance to emerge upon our horizon, and our responses reveal how shifty our confidence in God actually is.

The cure for an anxious disposition is a good memory. God has displayed consistent faithfulness through the pages of Scripture and throughout the years of your life. At every juncture of your life, God has exhibited consistent reliability. Even if he didn't move in the way you anticipated, he still moved nonetheless. You know how I know that? You are still here. The very evidence that you are reading this sentence means that God has kept you. That single fact should inject bravery into your soul because you know who walks with you.

When you reach the next impossible set of circumstances, you need to take a trip down memory lane.

Remind yourself of how God delivered you each time you were in dire situations. Look back and remember how he did the impossible time after time. Recount that battle when impending circumstances engulfed you, and yet, all of a sudden, God emerged on the scene, and the fight was subsequently over. Allow the power of God's Spirit to make you abound in hope yet again (Rom. 15:13). The battle isn't over until God says it is over, and his faithfulness guarantees that he is already in the fight.

The beauty of God's faithfulness also lies in the fact that no one is forcing him to be present in our lives. I have known people who showed up for duty because they had to make an appearance or else they would suffer the consequences. Who could threaten God with any type of repercussion if he failed to deliver? God is faithful because he wants to be faithful. He is not begrudgingly coming to your aid, but he is eagerly bounding to the rescue.

The priest Samuel made it a habit to remember God's faithfulness in the past to help him move forward. During a pivotal episode in Israel's history, their enemies drew close to slow down their progress. Samuel picked up a stone and set it before the people as a tangible monument. He named the stone, "Ebenezer" (1 Sam. 7:12). The name means "thus far God has helped us." This stone of remembrance was placed to reinvigorate Israel's faith. At a halfway marker along their journey, they needed to be reminded of God's faithfulness in the past. It reoriented their perspective. In the middle of where you've been and where you're going, it's helpful to remember who has been there every step of the way. Like Samuel, we have plenty of past episodes and future uncertainties to unnerve us. We can only counteract legitimate anxiety with robust theology. You're not there yet, but take a meaningful glance down at every Ebenezer in your life to remind yourself of how far you have come. If the LORD has helped me this far, how could I fathom that he would leave me now?

Even if you are currently struggling, remind yourself regarding the faithfulness of God. Has God delivered you? Has he shown up for you in the midnight hours? Did he come through when you thought there was no way? I bet he has. If you listed out all of God's miraculous deeds that he has done in your life, your mind would combat that ruthless anxiety, and your soul would be free to worship. God is faithful. You can trust in him when there is nothing else to trust.

✂ FAITHFULNESS REVIEW

Incorrect Perception: ~~God is unreliable.~~

Correct Attribute: *God is faithful.*

Definition: *The faithfulness of God means that whatever God says is entirely true and it will truly come to pass.*

Focal Verse: *If we are faithless, he remains faithful – for he cannot deny himself (2 Tim. 2:13).*

Implication: *Due to God's unwavering faithfulness, we can completely trust him no matter what comes our way.*

🗔 FURTHER STUDY

What concept from this chapter encouraged your soul?

Meditate on 2 Thessalonians 3:1-5. What does Paul's prayer request reveal about God's faithfulness?

How did God's faithfulness intersect with the Thessalonian believers' activity (2 Thess. 3:4)?

📋 **CORRECTIVE** THEOLOGY

How could we allow disappointments with the unfaithfulness of others taint our perception of the faithful God?

What examples in your life do you have concerning God's faithfulness in the past that give you hope for the future?

If you had complete confidence in the faithfulness of God, what would you change today due to being convinced of his promises?

CHAPTER 13
THE GRADE-ON-A-CURVE GOD

After every test taken within the halls of academia, at least one student is praying that the teacher will graciously grade on a curve. Due to a lack of preparation or a believed impossible standard, the student just hopes that enough of his classmates did as poorly as he thought he did that the teacher will be forced to bump all grades up. If the highest score were an 85, then all students would receive an additional 15-point curve which might ensure that some students live to procrastinate yet another day.

Much like that teacher, many people are praying that God grades on a curve. The cosmic test is difficult and thorough, and we are in desperate need of assistance in order to pass. Throughout life, an individual realizes that he is not the most upright being in the world. He understands that to be welcomed in heaven, he's going to need some help. He believes that he's not as bad as everyone else, but he's not the most righteous either. If God requires an A+, he's hoping that the Grade-on-a-Curve God comes through and bumps up everyone's score. Surely he will level the playing field, right?

The legalist correlation trap is a subtle yet severe danger. Since we are painfully aware of our unholiness, we would rather intentionally point out everyone else who is worse than us. It seems more advantageous for us to refocus God's attention to their rampant sin rather than addressing our unfortunate issues. Holiness based on comparison is not a noteworthy goal in our culture. To be holier than most of those around you may not be that impressive of a feat. Even if God granted a significant curve for most of us, would it be enough?

The belief that God judges us on a scale compared to others is rampant and rampantly wrong. There exist two pivotal problems with this prominent view of God: 1) God doesn't grade on a curve, and 2) Jesus is the supreme curve-buster anyway. God demands holiness, and Jesus provided it. Jesus came as God wrapped in human flesh and lived perfectly for his entire life. If we were hoping for a curve, Jesus robbed us of that possibility.

God does not grade on a curve. God is holy.

THE HOLINESS OF GOD

The task of defining holiness is an infinitely arduous task in of itself. While we tend to think of holiness as referring to something sacred, it really implies that something is set apart from something else. If holiness is to reveal the set apart nature of something, then God is the definition of holiness.

God's holiness means that he is entirely distinct from everything else in creation. God is holy. He is utterly unlike any other. While history records multiple ethnicities showing devotion to numerous deities, the God of the Bible claims to be in a category all by himself. Fundamentally, no other gods actually exist. Practically, many other gods do exist. The holiness of God demands a uniqueness that can be rivaled by no other.

As Moses began to sing beside the recently subsided Red Sea, he proclaimed this line over the dry Israelites: "Who is like you, O LORD, among the gods? Who is like you, majestic in holiness, awesome in glorious deeds, doing wonders?" (Exod. 15:11). With their enemies recently engulfed by the adjacent waters, the power of their gods was drowned as well. In those days, when two armies went to war, the accompanying gods were seen as the heavyweights duking it out above the squadrons on the battlefield. A victorious army revealed a mightier god than the other. What was unique about the Israelites was their claim that their God was holy. He was set apart from the rest of the pack. Not only was their God victorious, but he was also in a league all unto himself. For when the Israelites won a battle, it was rarely with swords, spears, and arrows, but rather, they experienced victory by waters (Exod. 14:27), trumpets (Josh. 6:20), and jars (Judg. 7:19). Who is like this God? No one else! He is holy. He is utterly and uniquely distinct.

Morally, God's holiness means that he is without a trace of sin. God is set apart morally. He is incapable of sinning because sin contradicts his nature. God's set apart identity demands a set apart activity. He is not like a sinful man (Num. 23:19). Isaiah's fear in God's presence came from the fact that he was an unholy person living among unholy people, and he was now dreadfully in the presence of the Holy One (Isa. 6:5). God is not only holy, but Isaiah learned something significant from the mouths of the seraphim. God is holy, holy, holy (Isa. 6:3). In John's vision, he saw other heavenly beings repeating the same distinction to the third degree (Rev. 4:8). Scripture never records another instance of attributing God to another threefold status, but these beings deemed it necessary. No one ever says that God is love, love, love. No one claims him to be wise, wise, wise. Yet these angels declare him to be holy, holy, holy. God isn't only set apart. He is set apart, set apart, set apart. God is other than, other than, other than. His holiness is so complete that the saints of old presumed themselves dead when they encountered it (Rev. 1:17).

Qualitatively, God's holiness means that he is awfully separate from us. While we typically use awful to describe something as unpleasant, the word initially implied something full of awe. Encountering something awful meant it produced a type of unique reverential wonder and fearful inspiration from which it was hard to recover.

God is so holy that he cannot view the heavens as wholly pure (Job 15:15). Does that mean that God is so sacred that even the heavens fail to be adequately pure in his presence? That's precisely what Scripture teaches. He is so set apart that heavenly places and godly people fail to maintain their claims to holiness in his presence. In the presence of the Holy One, the moon is not bright, the stars are not pure, and mankind is not worthy (Job 25:5). In his presence, people are comparatively on the scale of a maggot or a worm (Job 25:6). He is so holy that none of us can even claim to possess adequate knowledge regarding him (Prov. 30:3).

Devotionally, God's holiness means that he is singularly committed to his glory. From everlasting, God has been holy and wholly committed to his plans (Hab. 1:12). As the only genuinely holy one, God is willing and able to instill some of his sacredness upon the Sabbath day, the Levitical order, and the tabernacle construction. God has been in the business of making unholy things holy.

While he must allow imperfection in his presence or else we would never encounter him, he still reminds us of the glaring difference between him and us. In God's presence, the holiest of men even found the need to remove their shoes due to God's stifling holiness (Exod. 3:5; Josh. 5:15). He is so holy that even the dirt becomes holy in his presence. As a holy nation of priests (1 Pet. 2:9), we are to be committed to being singularly committed to his glory as well. We are to "strive for peace with everyone, and for the holiness without which no one will see the Lord" (Heb. 12:14).

Not only is God the definition of holiness, but God is also the indicator of holiness. When people encounter God in the Bible, it was a dreadful thing. Notice that I did not say it was a bad thing but a dreadful thing. When unholy people encounter a holy God, a great sense of needed fear accompanies that moment. While it can rattle us to the core, we require that fear to wake us up as rebellious insurrectionists who wrongfully seek to be the center of the universe. We need moments of realization to remind us that we aren't able to handle such a central position.

The encounters in the Bible set the table for us. When God spoke to Moses from the burning bush, Moses hid his face "for he was afraid to look at God" (Exod. 3:6). Such terror and awe gripped his soul when he realized that he was in the presence of the Almighty! When Joshua, the commander of Israel's army, encountered a mysterious figure, the commander of the LORD's army, he fell down before him (Josh. 5:14). For those who think this figure was an angel, think again. Anytime that an angel is worshiped, the angels correct the mistake (Rev. 19:10;

22:9). With Joshua, this commander instructs the worshiper to take off his sandals because he is on holy ground (Josh. 5:15). The only other time we see that is at the burning bush. This commander is no angel. Joshua knew it, and he responded appropriately. Many years later, when Saul was blinded by just the mere light of God, he fell to the ground (Acts 9:4) and refused to eat or drink for three days (Acts 9:9). He was overwhelmed by what he could only see for a moment.

If those expressions depict what happens in the world, you would imagine that the scene in heaven is different. The approved proximity to God should reveal an aura of familiarity with his holiness, but apparently, it does not. Shockingly, it seems as if the responses in heaven of more holier figures are even more extreme than those below. Angelic beings arrayed with six wings require two of them to cover their face in the presence of God (Isa. 6:2). On repeat, they declare God's unique holiness to the third power (Isa. 6:3). In the throne room of heaven, twenty-four thrones flank the great throne (Rev. 4:4). While some might question the identity of who claim those seats of honor, none will disagree regarding the magnitude of the prestige itself. If throughout history, God chooses only twenty-four individuals to sit upon special thrones and wear exquisite crowns in heaven, you would assume their disposition to be that of distinguished confidence. Not so at all! As soon as God enters the room, the who's who of heaven fall down before him and cast their crowns before him (Rev. 4:10). Their mantra is not, "we are worthy," but "worthy are you, our Lord and God, to receive glory and honor and power" (Rev. 4:11). Even the holy angels of heaven fall down in the presence of God (Rev. 7:11).

THE AWE WE NEED

Our souls are wired to require awe. In the holiness of God, we finally arrive at the stupefying splendor of which we were destined to behold. God is the magnificent majesty that is the needed remedy to get our poisoned eyes off of our sickening selves. His glory should bring an alarming reckoning to our spirits as it puts us on notice to wake up to our apathetic attitude. Our frivolous nature of approaching God on our own terms is an offense to the holiness of God. When will we wake up to the immense quality of his glorious uniqueness? We are not equals with him. We cannot approach him on our own terms. If we dare approach him, we must approach the throne of grace with confidence in Jesus, the great high priest (Heb. 4:16), not in us the unholy transgressors. God is the standard of holiness. He does not reach up to some standard above him. He will not stoop to some expectation beneath him. The measure even derives from within himself. "The fear of the LORD is the beginning of wisdom, and the knowledge of the Holy One is insight" (Prov. 9:10). To understand holiness, we must comprehend God.

If we only speak of God as gracious, we belittle him. God's grace is more extensive than our capacity for a scandalous imagination, but it is not so cheap that it fails to expect a standard of holiness. If we render God so gracious that he cannot establish moral lines, we have gone too far.

God's holiness is needed to be so intense to make his grace so amazing.

We cannot experience the grace of God if we do not first wrestle with the holiness of God. We must not fear to declare the standard, we should fear that we are unable to meet it. The Church can no longer articulate immorality because we think God will not call it out. We are wrong! In our ever-increasingly tolerant culture, we feel as if it is not anyone's responsibility to define sin. I would agree that it is not my job to define sin, but it is my job to distinguish sin. If God calls something unholy, it is unholy. As people who are called to be temples filled with the presence of God, we must remember that we are no longer our own and unable to live however we hold to be sinfully convenient (1 Cor. 6:19). When God's people refuse even attempting to pursue a type of skimpy holiness, we resort to standardizing an unholy worldliness. Some believers look so much like non-believers that it is hard to distinguish between the two.

God's holiness consumes any unholiness near him. He is a consuming fire (Heb. 12:29). No one or nothing is safe from the unquenchable flames of his holiness. When the godless grasp the holiness of God, fearful trembling will seize their souls. How can any of us "dwell with the consuming fire" (Isa. 33:14)? The fact is that none of us can. He is holy, and we are incapable of ever reaching his standard of holiness.

If God is that holy and we are this unholy, how can we ever find the required reconciliation? If the chasm is that far between us, there is nothing we can do to repair the gap. In truth, we could never lessen the divide, but God could in a unique and unexpected way. God is the provider of holiness.

God doesn't soften his standard of holiness, but he supplies the cost for our unholiness. Through holy Jesus living a holy life before his holy Father, he is able to take the penalty for our unholiness and transform us into holy people. He pays the price for our unholy rebellion and changes us into holy disciples.

Legally, we are made holy by the sacrifice of Jesus. "We have been sanctified through the offering of the body of Jesus Christ once for all" (Heb. 10:10). Being sanctified means being made holy. The sacrifice of Jesus on the cross can provide the needed holiness for unholy people once and for all. It is not producing temporal holiness, but his sacrifice procures eternal holiness. We do not reach a status of holiness based upon our works, for they are too unholy (Eph. 2:9). We obtain a standard of holiness because the works of Jesus were utterly holy. Justification is the moment when God Almighty slams the gavel down in the courtroom of redemption and claims that his children are no longer guilty. As criminals against the King, the cross made us justified judicially before his throne and welcomed into his home.

Practically, we are becoming holy by the support of Jesus. Once we understand that our records are forever clean legally, we want to experience that freedom practically. We no longer have to be conformed to the passions of our former ignorant manner of life (1 Pet. 1:14). God expects us to be holy. Why? We are to be holy because he is holy (1 Pet. 1:16). Set yourself apart, for we serve a God who is set apart, set apart, set apart. We failed the test for which there was no curve, but Jesus exchanged our papers with his. We are now equipped and encouraged to walk in a manner worthy of our calling (Eph. 4:1). We live out holiness as a proof of our redemption but never as a prerequisite.

✂ HOLINESS REVIEW

Incorrect Perception: ~~God grades on a curve.~~

Correct Attribute: *God is holy.*

Definition: *God's holiness means that he is entirely distinct from everything else in creation.*

Focal Verse: *There is none holy like the LORD; there is none besides you; there is no rock like our God (1 Sam. 2:2).*

Implication: *God's holiness should rescue us from a mediocre devotion.*

🗔 FURTHER STUDY

What about God's holiness mesmerizes you?

Meditate on Isaiah 6:1-8. From this passage, what proper responses to God's holiness do we see?

Why is Isaiah's willingness to go (Isa. 6:8) significant regarding the progression of his vision?

CORRECTIVE THEOLOGY

What are the signs that we have gotten used to the holiness of God?

What about God's unique holiness should change the way that we interact with him?

If we are unable to imitate perfectly the standard of holiness that God deserves, why should we even attempt it? How do we try?

CHAPTER 14
THE SHADY PAST GOD

You really want to give that wish-washy person a second chance, but you are relatively confident that a second chance was utilized a long time ago. All of us have known that person who is trying to get a clean slate and experience a fresh start. While you want to give the individual the benefit of the doubt, experience alerts you to the fact that this person is probably unable to be trusted again. If you look back over the past, there is simply just too much wreckage along the road. The dark past clouds up a potential future too much. You hope that the person can turn things around, but you just assume that the immense amount of wrongdoings in the past will hinder him or her from ever actually living an honest life.

Many people believe that God has a shady past. He possibly received that reputation not in the manner of missteps but by miscalculations. We discover this line of thinking every time someone speaks of being angry with God. The incessant questioning of his reasoning and the lingering skepticism regarding his decisions reveal that we aren't entirely sure he has always done the right things. We want to trust him for the here and now, but we are too conflicted by the there and then. We are plagued with questions regarding the drunk driver, the cancer diagnosis, the estranged loved one, and the throbbing heartache. Despite the fact of all the good God has done, we are still left wondering if he always does the right thing. In questioning his decisions, we judge his heart. Based upon the status of our current situations, his past lingers into our present.

God does not have a shady past. God is righteous.

THE RIGHTEOUSNESS OF GOD

We believe that God has the power to do all things, but do we think that he does all things right? If God can perform subpar, that implies that he is imperfect. If he is flawed, he cannot be God. We must establish the rightness of God's actions or else all standards of right and wrong reach an anarchical conclusion.

The righteousness of God means that God always does what is right according to his standard. God's record never archives a misstep because there never was one. He has always done what was right, he is currently doing what is right, and he will forever do what will be right. Since God is immutable, we do not have to fear that his standard of correctness is elusive. God defines what is right and doing what is right according to his ideal means that he has a more reliable and lofty prospect with which to establish the needed standard of rightness. The tides of cultural change cannot improve that which is already perfect. Even if a culture thinks God's way is wrong, he is still right. Despite if an individual challenges his process, God's way will prove the best path in the end.

God is righteous. He always does right. He never ever does wrong. "For the LORD is righteous; he loves righteous deeds; the upright shall behold his face" (Ps. 11:7). Since he is righteous, he absolutely adores when others do righteous deeds (Ps. 33:5; 37:28). When God feels indignation as he beholds the blatant unrighteousness of the world, he confirms his status as the only righteous judge (Ps. 7:11). Beyond actions, he can behold the motives. As the righteous God, he alone can establish people as righteous because he can search our hearts and our minds (Ps. 7:9).

Our Heavenly Father is perfect in every way (Matt. 5:48). Maintaining moral perfection, he also displays practical perfection since every one of his methods is perfect (Ps. 18:30). Even his Law that he composed is perfect (Ps. 19:7). His Word can revive the soul and illuminate the simple. As you read his Word, you might be challenged by his ledger. His past has quite a few moments that might require a further review from the booth. Consistent with God's character, no part of his history shames him. Even the actions that seem controversial were the best and right thing to do. God unashamedly claims credit for many moments that we find difficult to swallow.

God is not ashamed regarding a single moment from his past.

When God allowed the brothers of Joseph to beat, discard, and profit from his enslavement, was that good? I am sure Joseph found it difficult to perceive the rightness as he endured through those events. Joseph must have thought that God should have stepped in and stopped the proceedings, but instead, God allowed all of it to transpire. The claim that God was with Joseph (Gen. 39:2) might have seemed laughable as he was trafficked, seduced, accused, imprisoned, and forgotten. Years later, as Joseph's brothers were all about to die from famine, we realize that God had done the right thing by placing Joseph in a position of authority to keep the family alive. The Messiah was coming from Judah's line (Gen. 49:10), and so this family would not die in starvation. God was using Joseph to sustain his plan. Joseph gladly accepted his role in the process. "As for you, you meant evil against me, but God meant it for good, to bring it about that many people should be kept alive, as they are today" (Gen. 50:20). They did wrong, but God was still doing right.

When God commanded the bloody wars of Joshua to take the land for the Israelites, was that good? It's one thing to win the region, but it's another to devote everything within it to destruction (Josh. 6:17). The razing of buildings, the ravaging of fields, and the slaughtering of inhabitants seems so barbaric and unnecessary. Just allow them to win the battle and settle into the land. Don't miss out on the opportunities and resources that could advance these newly formed people.

It wasn't long before the Israelites realized why the land's devastation was so important. Achan took some of the devoted things for himself (Josh. 7:1). What was supposed to be devoted to complete destruction was dedicated for personal benefit. Among the treasury was remnants of idolatrous practices that would prove to infect the soul of Israel. At the end of their conquest, Joshua was still aware of lingering gods polluting their religious devotion (Josh. 24:14). This tolerant allowance of sin led to a nation where everyone did what was right in their own eyes (Judg. 21:25). When the people were finally exiled from their home, it is revealed that they never entirely removed those false gods from their midst (2 Kgs. 17:7-8). What seemed like a shocking standard in Joshua's day made logical sense on eviction day. Once you remember that this nation was supposed to save the world from false religion by pointing to the one righteous God (Isa. 49:6), you realize how important it was for them to rid the land of idolatrous filth. How could they show the world the glories of God if they were still enamored with the glitter of idols?

When God allowed sinless Jesus to be brutally slaughtered upon a cross of which he did not deserve, was that good? The right thing was to put sinners like me on the cross and remove Jesus from it. Jesus never committed sin (1 Pet. 2:22), yet he became sin (2 Cor. 5:21). In Christ, there was no trace of transgression (1 John 3:5). Even one of the criminals crucified next to Jesus understood this truth. While one desired release, the other desired Jesus. The heaven-bound criminal proclaimed, "And we indeed justly, for we are receiving the due reward of our deeds; but this man has done nothing wrong" (Luke 23:41). The right thing to do was for him to suffer on the cross and for Jesus to be removed from the cross. Yet, Jesus endured the cross, despising the shame, and he has now seated at the right hand of God (Heb. 12:2). What seemed wrong at the time is the only right thing able to procure our salvation!

God is so righteous that it makes our righteousness appear like filthy rags before him (Isa. 64:6). "Our unrighteousness serves to show the righteousness of God" (Rom. 3:5). In our presence, he appears all the more glorious! Due to such a standard given by God and maintained through Jesus, none of us are able to endure. Yet there is grace! There is forgiveness! "If you, O LORD, should mark iniquities, O Lord, who could stand? But there is forgiveness with you, that you may be feared" (Ps. 130:3-4).

We are not able to retrieve this righteousness, but we can receive it. "The righteousness of God comes through faith in Jesus Christ for all who believe. For there is no distinction: for all have sinned and fall short of the glory of God, and are justified by his grace as a gift, through the redemption that is in Christ Jesus" (Rom. 3:22-24). Through the righteousness of Jesus, we have access to the righteousness we need to stand before God.

THE STANDARD WE NEED

God declares clearly what is right. Jesus performed flawlessly what was right. We struggle consistently with doing what is right. Part of our issue lies in the fact that we still live in a fallen world full of reprehensible reminders. This world is not what it should be. We suffer. We struggle. We agonize. It is burdensome to live out our calling when suffering challenges our steps. We know that Christ makes us righteous, but we strain to live out righteousness due to the struggles that come our way.

We often struggle with God's righteousness by asking the question, "Why do bad things happen to good people?" While it is a common question, one specific word significantly flaws the reasoning. The word "good" will always prove to be a dilemma when you attach it to describing the tricksy human race. No person is deemed as good or right (Rom. 3:10; Ps. 14:3; Luke 18:19). The only right person who ever lived was Jesus Christ. He was the only flawless one (1 Pet. 1:19), and yet he suffered immensely.

So if Jesus suffered for doing right, what should I expect for doing wrong? I shouldn't assume I will live a carefree life. Suffering is inevitable regardless of what is the responsible catalyst. I often want to know the cause of the misery I have to endure. Is my opposition from God, Satan, enemies, or my own consequences? If God is testing me, if Satan is tempting me, if enemies are trying me, or if consequences are troubling me, the end goal is all the same – let me not turn away from God during times of trouble.

While I understand the principle, I still find myself wanting to demand reasons for my situations. We rarely get an answer regarding the impetus of our suffering. Regardless of the origin of the difficulty, our reactions should be the same in each scenario. No matter the reasoning for our pain, we should strive to be found faithful through it.

By the time God informs us in eternity regarding the logic of our suffering, we will probably be too enthralled by him to care any longer.

While some of our theology struggles with thinking that God could initiate suffering, most Christians would believe that he at least allows it. That approach seems to be a more palatable position, but is it sufficient? Each of us will assume one of three scenarios regarding our suffering: 1) God did it, 2) God didn't stop it, or 3) God couldn't stop it. Let's unpack each of these with an illustration. Imagine a dad and his daughter playing ball in the front yard by a busy road. At some point, the daughter is going to get hit in the face with the ball very hard. Who is responsible for the wrongdoing?

In the first scenario, the dad intentionally throws the ball at her head and injures her. She is visibly hurt, and he is undeniably responsible. This scenario illustrates the belief that God deliberately introduces suffering into our lives. He is responsible for it. The injury hurts, and God forthrightly takes the credit. If you believe that God is ultimately responsible for your suffering, you might be troubled with the lingering suspicion that he is uncaring.

In the second scenario, a bad person comes in and takes the ball to throw at the daughter. The father is present but doesn't stop the ball from hitting her. An evil person throws it, the father allows it, and the daughter is unfortunately hurting. This scene illustrates the belief by many people that God doesn't produce the suffering, but he doesn't stop it either. Either the devil or other people are the ones hurting us, but God ultimately allows it to happen. If you believe that God is passive during suffering, you are troubled that he seems unconcerned.

In the third scenario, a bad person throws a ball to hit the daughter, and the father is unable to stop it. Attempting to block it from hitting her, he is out of reach and out of time. Someone throws it, the father can't stop it, and the daughter is unfortunately hurt. This scenario illustrates the belief that God wants to prevent suffering but is regrettably unable. He currently has too much on his plate or incapable of pushing back the forceful foes fighting against us. If you believe that God is helpless during suffering, you might be troubled that he seems unable to come to your aid.

Which one is it? If God is uncaring, I question his motives. If God is unconcerned, I suspect his heart. If God is unable, I question his power. While the third scenario frightens me, the second option is the safe approach, I believe that often the first scenario is the most viable. It seems most appropriate if God remains in control even amidst our pain. As we imagine each of these scenarios, you might have missed something essential that only the father could see – the oncoming traffic. They were playing in the yard by a busy road. While our imaginative eyes fixate on the ball and on the daughter, we never ask the question about the road. In each of these scenarios, this little girl is dangerously close to oncoming traffic.

What if in the first scenario the father can see something to which the daughter is oblivious? What if an oncoming truck is coming over the hill? What if the only option he has to save her in a timely fashion is to hit her in the head with the ball and correct her direction before she fatally stumbles into the road?

What if, out of love, the father is willing to injure his child with lesser pain in order to save her from greater pain? The father isn't unloving then. He is doing the most loving thing he can do at that moment by pummeling his daughter in the face with a ball as fast as he can throw it. Hurting her is the right thing to do. Only the child who can trust that her father knows best can expect him to always do right even if it feels like he has done her wrong.

Sometimes it is challenging to trust in the fact that God is doing all things rightly. It doesn't feel as if it is fair, and it might never feel that way this side of eternity. We are living off of heavenly principles in an earthly system. We cannot obtain a fitting perspective from our vantage point. Only God who can see the whole picture and the entire timeline can ascertain the rightness of a situation. With the firestorms surrounding us, we have to trust that when the ash settles, God's ways will prove to be right. God's timing will reveal to be right. God's heart will prove to be the rightest right this world has ever rightly seen. Until that day when it proves correct, trust that it is right. Be patient to behold the a-ha moment that all of history has been longing to see. For once it comes, you will wonder why you ever struggled to trust him in the first place.

✂ RIGHTEOUSNESS REVIEW

Incorrect Perception: ~~God has a shady past.~~

Correct Attribute: *God is righteous.*

Definition: *The righteousness of God means that God always does what is right according to his standard.*

Focal Verse: *For the LORD is righteous; he loves righteous deeds; the upright shall behold his face (Ps. 11:7).*

Implication: *I never have to fear if God will handle a situation rightly or not.*

📄 FURTHER STUDY

What specific thought from this chapter made you think?

Meditate on Genesis 50:15-21. How did Joseph view God's involvement among his brother's treachery?

How does this passage interact with Romans 8:28?

# CORRECTIVE THEOLOGY

If every person in society had the same right to define what was right, how would that produce chaos among us?

Why is God's standard of rightness needed among all people?

What situation in your life do you wish that you understood better right now? How does it force you to rely on God's righteousness?

CHAPTER 15
THE PUSHOVER GOD

While each of us knows what it is like to walk on pins and needles around that strict authoritative figure in our lives, most of us also had a pushover or two around us for which we were eternally grateful. Whether it was a parent, grandparent, teacher, coach, or boss, we inevitably gravitated towards that person who was ever so graciously letting us off the hook. Even when our actions were shameful, we looked for that person whom we could manipulate and hoped that our mournful looks and sincere apologies spared us for yet another day of mischievous troublemaking. The pushovers in our lives allowed us to continue misbehaving without having to make any behavioral alterations.

Many people believe that God is the supreme pushover when it comes to mankind. Since God is regularly described as the most gracious being in the entire universe, we struggle to fathom how he could legitimately be mad at any of us for long. If we do the right set of penitent actions, God will forget about the justice we deserve and shower us with the grace we desire. In an attempt to rest in his amazing grace, we avoid contemplating his strict justice. God's judgment should only be reserved for that type of diabolical psychopath who is consistently bent on evil. Surely, he will overlook our variety of reputable missteps along the way. Are my "tolerable" sins really that evil? Our hope is errantly built on the chance that God will be a pushover regarding our comparatively trivial transgressions. We fail to realize that there are no insignificant transgressions against a significant God.

God is not a pushover. God is just.

THE JUSTICE OF GOD

Anselm of Canterbury was an Italian monk who was born in the 11th century. His work in theology and philosophy greatly assisted the Church. He once posed a valid question to God: "How dost thou spare the wicked if thou art just, supremely just?"

His question demands an answer. Discovering the biblical answer is vital to our personal theology as we wrestle with a doctrine of such potential magnitude. Our quandary is not determining how God will let some of those sinners off the hook, but why he would let any of us sinners off the hook.

The justice of God means that he has unique and incontestable rights to determine the rewards and consequences for every person. While we each seek to be judge, jury, and executioner, only God has the exclusive rights to determine what is appropriate and what is inappropriate. No matter how much we stretch out reaching for the fruit of that forbidden tree, that produce is not ours to possess (Gen. 2:17).

Not only are his rights for justice unique, but they are also incontestable. No one can argue when the gavel of God drops. No petition can sway him differently. There is not an assembly powerful enough to veto his decision. He is the determiner of eternal rewards and consequences for all people. Unbiasedly, God looks on the motives and actions of every person and delivers resolved judgment with no room for error or no need for deliberation. For every crime committed, God can handle each criminal justly.

Regarding the justice of God, we must realize that the standard comes from his character. Using that standard, God provided the Law contained within the Scriptures. Every person has broken that Law and invariably committed numerous offenses against God. Due to our transgressions, we deserve punishment, and God's punishment always fits the crime. While all of this information does seem like unfortunate news, there is a gracious atonement available for the penalty. All of these components are necessary for biblical theology. Any element removed from the weight of God's justice attempts to turn God into a dangerously weak pushover or a supremely harsh tyrant.

If God is just, where does the standard come from? The justice of God implies that he is the standard for truth himself. He doesn't bend to a standard, or else the standard would be higher than him. A standard outside of him would imply that it came from a different source. If he was forced to follow the rules of another, he is not the highest being. Regarding justice, God is the actual criterion.

"Surely, God will not act wickedly, and the Almighty will not pervert justice" (Job 34:12). God's standard and character are reliably viewed as "The Rock! His work is perfect, for all his ways are just; a God of faithfulness and without injustice, righteous and upright is he" (Deut. 32:4). Every single one of his ways is just and forever will be! He is utterly incapable of being unjust. Injustice hasn't the slightest opportunity even to stand in his presence. It wilts away amid his unbending standard of justice.

Since God is the Judge of all the earth, it makes sense that he would always do what is just (Gen. 18:25). Every decision and deed that belongs to him are upright (Ps. 92:15). As the King of kings, righteousness and justice are the very foundation of his throne (Ps. 97:2). Don't miss the imagery here. God grants kingship to himself, and no antagonist can dare rival his throne. Yet as he sits upon it, justice is the very foundation for how he rules. History has archived the accounts of dictatorial kings who expected justice for everyone in the kingdom except for the one upon the throne. Scandal and injustice in some way plague every palace's throne room throughout the ages. In many cases, justice would be delivered from the authority of an individual king, but many rulers would seek to avoid punishment for themselves regarding the injustice of which they were responsible. Only God's administration would house justice as the foundation of the throne. He has never been called on the carpet for unjust deeds. Justice is the standard by which he rules, and that standard comes from himself.

Since God is the actual standard for justice, he communicates that very standard to mankind through the Law. The justice of God is revealed through the specific laws he has delivered to the human race. Through the moral laws impressed upon our hearts and the written laws recorded within the Scriptures, we cannot claim ignorance regarding God's expectations. He has made them abundantly clear to our consciences.

Regarding the moral laws given to us, God's "eternal power and divine nature, have been clearly perceived, ever since the Creation of the world, in the things that have been made. So they are without excuse" (Rom. 1:20). An inherent moral compass has been placed upon every single one of our hearts, and regardless of which culture we originate, we discover common standards of right and wrong even if we violate it. As if the moral laws were insufficient, God has also given us clear instructions in his Word regarding how we are to live. We are to follow his rules with our manner of life because he is the LORD our God (Lev. 18:4).

God's rules are perfect and completely righteous (Ps. 19:9). All of the rules given by him are for his glory and for our good. So when God draws a line in the sand, there is always a justified reason for it. God says that he "will make justice the line, and righteousness the plumb line" (Isa. 28:17). A plumb line is a tool used for centuries by different types of builders. While in the middle of a construction project, it is difficult to determine accurate horizontal and vertical lines without basing them on previously laid materials. The plumb line is a cord with a weight attached to the end so that when it dangles freely, gravity reveals consistent angles. The standard of gravity exposed by the plumb line is more accurate, consistent, and trustworthy than the seasoned yet flawed construction worker's efforts thus far. With this imagery, we see the importance of God's justice. God is the standard of moral gravity that pulls every single decision into an evaluation. Through his written Word, every person can judge their wavering actions by his consistent standard.

Since God's standard of justice provides the Law as a plumb line, what happens if and when they are disobeyed? The offense of breaking God's commandments is severe condemnation. The justice of God means that he has an unrelenting and rightful judgment for when those laws are transgressed. God does not play favorites among transgressors. He has never been soft on certain individuals. He is not more lenient on specific races, genders, or socioeconomic classes. God will never be swayed by religious devotions or sorrowful promises. If sin has been committed, his judgment is categorically impartial. None of us have a chance to skirt by unnoticed.

"For the LORD your God is God of gods and Lord of lords, the great, the mighty, and the awesome God, who is not partial and takes no bribe. He executes justice" (Deut. 10:17-18). In our culture, many will declare that God's ways represented within the pages of the Bible are no longer just. The people in Ezekiel's day held the same mindset. "Yet you say, 'The way of the Lord is not just.' Hear now, O house of Israel: Is my way not just? Is it not your ways that are not just?" (Ezek. 18:25). Whenever justice is done, "it is a joy to the righteous but terror to evildoers" (Prov. 21:15). "For he who does wrong will receive the consequences of the wrong he has done, and that without partiality" (Col. 3:25). When the offense has been made, justice has been promised.

The justice of God guarantees that every wrong committed will be wholly punished. None of us can avoid this reality. God doesn't play with sin. There are no cute or playful sins in his book. "For whoever keeps the whole law but fails in one point has become guilty of all of it" (Jas. 2:10). Even if you think your sins are not as despicable as another, the fact that you are a sinner puts you in the same category as all the rest of us. The wages of sin is death (Rom. 6:23), and the destination for sinners is hell. No one can escape this verdict by his or her own power.

The LORD proclaims that he loves justice and hates injustice. He promises to give sinners their recompense (Isa. 61:8). As thoroughly encompassing are his judgments against all sinners, we can expect his unwavering consistency. He won't let transgressions simply slide under his radar. All of his decisions are true and just (Rev. 16:7). To maintain that measure, he is unable to soften his expectations. If he lowered his standards for one, he could no longer hold any of us to those expectations.

If God is the standard, and he has communicated it to us through the Law, what will our punishment be for the great offenses we have accumulated upon our records? I have good news for you today – you don't have to pay for your penalty because someone was willing to pay it for you! The justice of God ensures that no sinner's punishment can be avoided, but it can be atoned. At the cross of Jesus, we see that God's justice and God's mercy are not two conflicting traits within God, but they are two complimenting attributes of God.

Justice was served for the heaven-bound believer upon the wounds of the heaven-sent Savior.

How can God be both good and just? Such complexity calls some religions to have different gods carry out the two seemingly polarized emotions and actions. Hinduism will communicate the need to thank good, benevolent gods and to appease bloodthirsty, malevolent gods. In the Christian faith, these two apparently warring enemies befriend one another at the cross. In Jesus' willing sacrifice, God is offering grace, and yet, through the punishment, he is maintaining justice. "It was to show His righteousness at the present time, so that He might be just and the justifier of the one who has faith in Jesus" (Rom. 3:26). Not only is God the just, but he is also the justifier. For those who have faith in Jesus, God's justice is satisfied in the substitutionary death of Jesus.

THE LINE WE NEED

As God's immense and unflinching standard of justice sweeps over the souls throughout history, this measurement has practical implications for us today. If I am not the standard of justice, then I must stop trying to be the avenger of transgressions against me. If someone has wronged me, it is not my responsibility to make it right. We are expected to leave the administration of justice into God's capable hands. "Beloved, never avenge yourselves, but leave it to the wrath of God, for it is written, 'Vengeance is mine, I will repay, says the Lord'" (Rom. 12:19). God will have all accounts settled in the end. Trust him to do his job in his time. His retribution will be just and timely.

In addition to the practical wisdom and patience that God's justice brings to our interpersonal relationships, it also provides the peace needed for our relationship with God. The death of Jesus satisfies God's requirement for our justice yet never violates it. Through his sacrifice, Jesus delivers us from the wrath to come (1 Thess. 1:10; 5:9). The believer does not need to live in fear of coming judgment if Jesus already settled the accounts. Through this justification, we are saved from his wrath since Jesus already experienced it. When Jesus comes, he will "inflict vengeance on those who do not know God and on those who do not obey the gospel of our Lord Jesus" (2 Thess. 1:8). Yet for those who have received the gospel, they will "be saved by him from the wrath of God" (Rom. 5:9).

In administering justice, we don't have to worry about God's outlook. God is not like us – he is not emotionally torn regarding what to do. We must not attempt to bring God down to our level (Ps. 50:21). He is returning one day to bring appropriate justice related to every person's individual response to the gospel (Matt. 25:32).

There exist only two categories of people. Every one of us will pay for our sins eternally, or Jesus has already paid for them entirely. For those rebelliously bent on receiving justice for eternity in hell, this life on planet Earth will be as close to heaven as they will ever experience. For those humbly receptive to trusting by faith for eternity in heaven, this life on planet Earth will be as close to hell as they will ever know. Has Jesus paid the penalty for you or does your record still show a debt of which you cannot afford? You don't have to die! God takes no pleasure in the death of the wicked and would instead have you turn back from your evil ways and live (Ezek. 33:11)!

The soul who sins will die (Ezek. 18:20), but God is eagerly desirous to show us grace. "Therefore the LORD longs to be gracious to you, and therefore, He waits on high to show mercy to you. For the LORD is a God of justice; blessed are all those who long for Him" (Isa. 30:18). His justice and mercy are satisfied in the person of Jesus. Thank God that, in Christ, we will not get what we deserve. "If we confess our sins, He is faithful and just to forgive us our sins and to cleanse us from all unrighteousness" (1 John 1:9). God is not a pushover. Sin must be paid, but Jesus has enough in his account to cover you. This mercy he delivers is free but not cheap. The payment your sins required was not overlooked in part but paid in full.

✂ JUSTICE REVIEW

Incorrect Perception: ~~God is a pushover.~~

Correct Attribute: *God is just.*

Definition: *The justice of God means that he has unique and incontestable rights to determine the rewards and consequences for every person.*

Focal Verse: *The Rock, his work is perfect, for all his ways are justice. A God of faithfulness and without iniquity, just and upright is he (Deut. 32:4).*

Implication: *God will resolve every situation with justice by the time of eternity.*

🗐 FURTHER STUDY

What particular thought from this chapter gave you hope?

Meditate on Hebrews 9:27-28. What is promised to every person after death? What does that mean?

At the final judgment, there will be a justice given or a justice recognized as already provided. What makes the difference for which you will receive?

📋 **CORRECTIVE** THEOLOGY

Why are we unable to approximate adequate justice for other people?

What makes God's unique perspective the only one able to administer true justice?

What situation do you need to resign as the avenger of wrongs?

CHAPTER 16
THE THUNDERBOLT GOD

Mythological stories and comic book narratives often include a thunderbolt-wielding figure ready to come out of the sky and wreak havoc upon the sniveling weaklings of humanity. Perched upon his birdseye throne, he can easily spot those pathetic lifeforms who need his lightning and his thunder to rid the world of their miserable existence. If you fare to live another day, never forget he is watching and waiting from above all the while looking for your slightest misstep so that he can blast you into oblivion. He possesses a superior power and a keen awareness to ascertain every person's intrinsic worth. The realization that he has such knowledge should keep you on your proverbial toes. With every rumble of thunder and every pop of lightning, he reminds you that your time might soon come.

Many people fear the Thunderbolt God. Utilizing cosmic powers to enforce universal karma, this entity is awaiting your next mistake with sadistic glee. Foaming at the mouth for you to step out of line, he is ready to drop the hammer as soon as he sees you falter. Every car crash, every bounced check, every relationship lost, every flu virus, and every testing trial is a reminder that God is watching you and ferociously eager to let you have it. For all the times you have bemoaned that you did not get what you deserved, weep no more. With this version of God, you will always get what you deserve, and you will not be happy with the results. With thunderbolts reigning from the sky into our lives, we must ever be aware that our next mistake may prove to be our last.

God is not the thunderbolt-wielder. God is merciful.

THE MERCY OF GOD

Before we go any further, we do need to establish that God doesn't mind striking the lightning and peeling the thunder when such elements are warranted. God's mercy does not mean that he is a weak grandparent too soft to call for punishment. God is still powerful enough and intentional enough to thunder his presence when he deems it necessary. God's voice thunders from heaven (Ps. 18:13; 29:3; Job 37:4-5; 40:9;). God sends out the lightning to do his bidding (Zech. 9:14; Job 38:35). It should not amaze us when God brings the thunderbolts, but when he refrains them. When God intervenes to get our attention, it is his justice, but whenever he interjects by giving us the unexpected, it is his mercy.

The mercy of God means that God does not give his children what they deserve. All of us have fallen short of God's standard (Rom. 3:23). The paycheck for our rebellion is nothing less than death (Rom. 6:23). Anything better than that is due to God's mercy. Praise be to the Merciful One because he is eager to give it! "Therefore the LORD longs to be gracious to you, and therefore he waits on high to show mercy to you" (Isa. 30:18). No one is forcing him to show us mercy! He has never begrudgingly offered freedom for the captive. The very heart of God is intensely longing to show mercy to us.

God's mercy is what causes us to "be born again to a living hope through the resurrection of Jesus Christ from the dead" (1 Pet. 1:3). If we could earn this salvation, it would not be mercy. We don't have enough good deeds in the tank anyway to provide the needed entry fee. "He saved us, not because of works done by us in righteousness, but according to his own mercy" (Titus 3:5). The only reason we know Jesus is not because we deserve it. On the contrary, it is precisely because we don't deserve it.

Our wayward ways guarantee consistent reliance on his mercy. "The steadfast love of the LORD never ceases; his mercies never come to an end; they are new every morning; great is your faithfulness" (Lam.

3:22-23). As ever-changing as our dedication is, his faithfulness is consistent as the rising sun. Every single morning, we receive new mercies! Due to our continual sin, we are always in need of such precious daily treasures. Yesterday's mercies aren't sufficient for today's transgressions. Thanks be to God who has yet to run out! Every dawn, he awakens us to marvelous new mercies.

The narrative of the Bible reveals our constant need for God's mercy. Throughout the pages, God's people do such atrocities that the reader assumes that God's mercies will eventually run out. Yet time and time again, he provides them with additional expressions of clemency. After the Israelites carved a golden calf to worship in the desert, God introduced this Exodus generation to his unbelievable mercy. While he should have departed from them and left them to fend for themselves in the harsh elements and dangerous surroundings due to their sin, he continued to prove his long-suffering commitment to the people. Once the dust had settled from the tragic rebellion, God gave Moses a description that would serve as cherished biographical information on the God they followed. "The LORD, the LORD God, merciful and gracious, slow to anger, and abounding in steadfast love and faithfulness" (Exod. 34:6).

The phrase must have stuck because, throughout the history of the Israelites, they kept repeating it at critical times for needed reassurance. When they arrived at the Promised Land, God reminded him that the reason they made it was because he had been merciful (Deut. 4:31). After King Hezekiah cleaned out the temple full of idolatrous filth, he believed that God's mercy was the only reason that they had not been consumed (2 Chr. 30:9). Isaiah noted that Israel's former troubles had been mercifully removed from God's sight (Isa. 65:16). The prophet Joel realized that even among the swarming locusts, God was exhibiting mercy that kept destruction limited (Joel 2:13). Even the psalmists contained the truth in their worship anthems. "The LORD is merciful and gracious, slow to anger and abounding in steadfast love" (Ps. 103:8).

The only reason we have hope is because God is a merciful God. At any moment, he is comprehensively justified in letting the thunderbolts fly. Throughout the pages of Scripture and the archives of our lives, God proves to prioritize mercy and exhibit long-suffering. Even our pleas for his return to restart this broken world is delayed due to his compassion. He is coming soon, but his delay is to allow more people the time to experience God's mercy (2 Pet. 3:9). Every day that he tarries, he is allowing people to experience the goodness of the LORD before it is too late (Ps. 27:13).

"All the paths of the LORD are mercy and faithfulness, for those who keep his covenant and his testimonies" (Ps. 25:10). As we follow him on this journey, the charted path declares mercy at every step. This compassionate God is abundant in mercy (Ps. 86:15). No one is forcing him to show it to us either.

God isn't begrudgingly offering mercy while pouting along the way.

Make no mistake about it, he delights in showering us with mercy (Mic. 7:18). His very purpose is to be merciful to those who don't deserve it (Jas. 5:11). "Mercy triumphs over judgment" (Jas. 2:13). God's mercy is so broad that it can overtake the deserving condemnation. We can approach the throne of God to receive mercy repeatedly because we have already been promised it assuredly (Heb. 4:16).

As those who have experienced God's compassion, it should change all of our interactions with others. The mercy and compassion that God shows us should be seen as contagious in our lives. Jesus displayed compassionate kindness towards the needy around him (Mark 6:34), and we are to reflect that in the way that we care for others. We are to be merciful since our Father is merciful (Luke 6:36). We will be blessed as we show mercy to others (Matt. 5:7). God's mercy is not only to be celebrated but also to be imitated.

THE COMPASSION WE NEED

This wondrous mercy is not a generous novelty; it is a necessary requirement. Without God's mercy, we are unable to be reconciled to him. Our sins render us deserving of judgment. No amount of excuses will suffice to rescue us from our eternal dilemma. How can we receive mercy if we deserve punishment?

Maybe it will help to illustrate the magnitude of such a concept. What does a woman deserve if she cheats on her husband? What should she receive if she has actually sold herself into prostitution and abandoned her family? She deserves estrangement. If she had been that unfaithful, most of us would warrant that she should get what she deserves. Now imagine if this woman was married to a godly and consistent preacher. What is she due? I believe most of us say that she merits to be divorced and forgotten. Allow her to experience all the depth of consequences she has chosen for her sinful trajectory.

Unfortunately, this scenario isn't a hypothetical situation. It was a painful reality for a prophet named Hosea, who married a prostitute named Gomer. When God commanded Hosea to marry her, he revealed that not only was she a prostitute, but she would continue to work as a prostitute as they established a family and a home. God was leading Hosea to flesh out a painful illustration of God's own relationship with his people. "Go, take to yourself a wife of whoredom and have children of whoredom, for the land commits great whoredom by forsaking the LORD" (Hos. 1:2).

Loving her despite her past is one thing, but loving her aware of her future is another. God informed Hosea that unfaithfulness would not be Gomer's past time indulgence. She would continue. Just like Hosea, God knew what he was getting into at the wedding altar with us, and yet he still showed up in the proper attire. If you read this account and balk at the thought of being required to imitate Hosea's example, you are missing the point. You are not meant to identify with Hosea; you are expected to identify with Gomer. We are not the ones loving the whore, we are the whores being loved. We are the unfaithful. We run around on God, and yet God is the one who still pursues us regardless of our promiscuous ways. He could have done so much better than us, and yet he still desires us all the way down to the altar.

As Hosea and Gomer have three children, it is implied that some of these do not even belong to Hosea, and yet he cares for them as his own. All the dysfunction present in this home does not deter him from scheduling the family photoshoot anyway. He is committed to her for whatever end. In a horrible twist, unfaithful Gomer eventually reaches the point that her prostitution winds her upon the slave table. She has been sex trafficked. Gomer's addiction to this lifestyle has gotten herself in serious trouble. Her waywardness has endangered her, and now she has become someone else's possession.

What should Hosea do? Gomer deserved harsh consequences, yet she received Hosea's abundant mercy. He did what God had already done for his people. Hosea ensured that he was the highest bidder for his unfaithful wife. Ironically, he has to pay for what already belongs to him. He rescues his bride from the slave table. "So I bought her for fifteen shekels of silver and a homer and a lethech of barley" (Hos. 3:2). Why is that significant? A slave's worth was typically registered as thirty shekels of silver (Exod. 21:32), which was a steep price. With Hosea only offering fifteen shekels of silver and other random contributions, it appears he doesn't possess the standard fee required. He is digging down into the couch cushions to find whatever it takes. Hosea has broken the bank on this purchase. In this purchase, Hosea wipes out his savings, clears his retirement, and strips his home of any remaining value. Why would he do that? Because he values his bride more. You never regret giving something of value for something you value more. This debt wasn't canceled; it was paid by another.

While slavery is never an ethically appropriate scenario, Gomer's recurring actions had bound her to a debt. She had played with fire for far too long, and now her actions left her smoldering among the ashes. Through her decisions, she became indebted. She essentially deserved the slave table, but instead, she received a welcoming home. She earned isolation, but she received intimacy. She was worth wrath, but she was given mercy. As he brings her back home, he reminds her, "You shall not play the whore, or belong to another man; so will I also be with you" (Hos. 3:3). As faithful as he has been to her, he still feels it necessary to remind her of his personal commitment yet again. He will be loyal to her regardless of how unfaithful she proves to be.

God never asked Hosea to do anything that he would not do. If you think Gomer's sin is treacherous, how would you define ours? Created in his image (Gen. 1:26-27), we were meant to bring him glory with our lives (Col. 1:16). We rebelled against him repeatedly (Rom. 3:23), causing our sins to separate us from him (Isa. 59:2). God demonstrated his love for us in that while we were still sinners, he sent Jesus to die for us (Rom. 5:8). He bought back what already belonged to him. The blood of Christ is the payment God was willing to give in order to purchase again those who previously belonged to him.

Oh, what mercy! What a costly sacrifice for ones so unworthy as I! After our consistent spiritual whoredom, you would imagine that Christ might go through the needed sacrifice but lacking the endearing affection through it. What marvels to consider – he actually went to the cross with joy (Heb. 12:2) because of his great love with which he loves us (Eph. 2:4). He is still looking forward to the wedding day even though we are way out of his league.

Scripture illustrates that the church, the people of God, is the Bride of Christ (Eph. 5:25-27; Rev. 19:7-9; 21:2, 9; Isa. 54:5; John 3:29). Jesus is the merciful groom, and God's people are his wayward bride. A wedding will take place, and somehow this bride will wear white. A bride wearing white is meant to symbolize her purity. It reveals that she has saved all of her love, affections, and devotion for her awaiting groom. If I take my sins and the sins of God's people from all time, I will dare argue that we should not be allowed in the building or at the altar. We are unfit to wear white to this service, and yet, that is the only appropriate color. Our garments will be fine, bright, and pure.

How can a bride so unfaithful dare to wear such white? Because the blood of the groom has made her garments white as snow (Ps. 51:7; Isa. 1:18). He loved her when she was unlovely (Eph. 2:5). He remained faithful when she was unfaithful (2 Tim. 2:13). He repurchased her when she already belonged to him (1 Pet. 1:19). She received mercy when she should have received wrath (Heb. 2:17). Despite the unfaithful behavior of this bride, she will wear white.

We deserved just abandonment but received unthinkable mercy. With this God, the thunderbolts have been thrown, but they have been absorbed by Jesus. He stood in our place. The price tag for our freedom has been paid in full, but our account is still intact. While we deserve judgment, we have been given mercy.

✂ MERCY REVIEW

Incorrect Perception: ~~God is the thunderbolt-wielder~~.

Correct Attribute: *God is merciful.*

Definition: *The mercy of God means that God does not give his children what they deserve.*

Focal Verse: *The steadfast love of the LORD never ceases; his mercies never come to an end; they are new every morning; great is your faithfulness (Lam. 3:22-23).*

Implication: *In Christ, God is unwilling to give you what you deserve.*

📄 FURTHER STUDY

What particular concept from this chapter encouraged you?

Meditate on Titus 3:3-7. According to this passage, for what are we responsible and for what is God responsible?

What reasoning for God's mercy do you find in this passage?

CORRECTIVE THEOLOGY

Why are we more prone to make it up to God rather than express our need for his mercy?

Why do we think that God is somehow grumpy about giving us mercy?

What traits should be exhibited from a life that has been blessed by the mercy of God?

CHAPTER 17
THE FUDDY-DUDDY GOD

You can spot a fuddy-duddy a mile away. Their pants are too high, their shoes are too outdated, their music is too quiet, and their schedule is too lame. Everywhere they go, these old-fashioned fossils just exude a boring traditionalism. As card-toting sticks-in-the-mud, their square conformist mentality flees from anything remotely fun or exciting.

Their frowns have been frozen in place, and wrinkles are developing as we speak just to make sure they don't wander off. The only adventure they seek is that of killing the adventures of others. If it can be enjoyed, it must be evil and avoided at all costs. These boring killjoys suck the fun out of life and cause many joyful people to pursue increasingly rebellious tendencies just to avoid becoming like them. Such a despondent demeanor seeks to take the pleasure out of everything for everybody.

Many people live as if God is the supreme fuddy-duddy. Referenced by those who took the fun out of fundamentalism, God is seemingly antagonistic towards anything enjoyable. If food, romance, music, games, or fellowship bring anything as diabolical such as laughter, smiles, or pep in your step, the curmudgeon Creator wants you to rid your life of such atrocities.

To their credit, many squares are aware of the debauchery that much of those things can lead to in our lives. Romantic appetites can lead to immoral lifestyles, trashy music can lead to despicable dispositions, greedy games can lead to disastrous downfalls, and unhealthy fellowship can lead to tragic decisions. Instead of addressing the matter of sinful directions, these individuals throw out the entire picture altogether. A hammer that can be used for good causes must be cast aside because it could possibly be used for wrong purposes. To have the propensity to cause such sin, it must be evil. Rid yourself of opportunities for such filth. God is way too serious for such trivial matters. A lighthearted moment is seen as an underhanded attack on the earnestness that one should consistently maintain.

God is not a fuddy-duddy. God is good.

THE GOODNESS OF GOD

In repairing our theology, we have to define goodness. We are not speaking of things that usher in mere delight. That definition is too limited for what we are considering. When I was a teenager, I would often hear well-meaning advisers tell me that those sinful people living in the world weren't having fun in their carousing endeavors. As I watched them, I begged to differ. Sin does produce pleasure. It just can only provide fun for a season. So just because something is fun does not mean that it is good. An uncomfortable medical exam is good if it alerts you to a serious diagnosis that needs to be addressed. While many things in this world bring enjoyment, God is the standard by which goodness must be defined.

The goodness of God means that he alone is the filter by which goodness is gauged. Everything God does is positive. Every part of who God is is exceptional. All things associated with his identity and activity are good. Since everything that he is and everything that he does is favorable, it reveals an appropriate approval of such a standard. By whose rule can we classify such things? It has to be his, of course. If God's goodness was voted upon among trifling people, we could never get an accurate evaluation. If his kindness were evaluated based upon our present feelings, we would never lockdown a sensible reading. If God's benevolence was contingent upon instant gratification, we might be left wanting.

Even the concept of goodness must imply that God determines what is right and what is wrong. No one is good except God alone (Mark 10:18). So the rest of us are left grasping for a standard of which we are painfully shy and unaware (Rom. 3:10). Since he is pure, it would make sense that the masterpieces made by his hands would be magnificent (Gen. 1:31). After each day's work, he reflected upon his cumulative production and repeatedly affirmed that its substance was inherently acceptable. It *was* good.

Despite common miscalculations, this God was fun by the way. He gave Adam the responsibility to name animals that he did not create and till a garden that he did not plant. None of the animals were dangerous. His work uniform proved that safety protocols were unnecessary during these carefree days. As if that wasn't enough, Adam woke up from a nap one day to behold uncensored Eve which quickly took the top ranking of all other things God had spectacularly created. God was good. Life was good. This paradise was the way that God originally intended life to be.

No wars existed. No sickness occurred. There was no waiting in line at the store. God had given this couple a paradise to enjoy, and they could enjoy it forever.

When people study the Garden of Eden, they usually complain about a particular tree positioned within the middle. Amidst the paradise given, God decided to plant a caveat to complicate matters. He didn't hide it behind a gate, but he placed it right there in front of their curious gazes. Here comes the Fuddy-Duddy God waving something in front of their faces of which they could not have. It must be something so good if it is to be that avoided. God had commanded that this first couple avoid only one source of produce. "And the LORD God commanded the man, saying, 'You may surely eat of every tree of the garden, but of the tree of the knowledge of good and evil you shall not eat, for in the day that you eat of it you shall surely die'" (Gen. 2:16-17).

As entitled independents, we would each balk at such a confining notion. How dare God deny them from that tree? As soon as God declared it off limits, it was the only tree that they desired. While we scratch our heads at God positioning a tree only to deny the first couple rights to it, we fail to miss a glaringly obvious admission on behalf of God. They could eat from all of the other trees within the garden. The single "thou shalt not" was encompassed by countless reminders of "thou shall." There was only one tree that was forbidden, and all other trees were encouraged. If they found an apple tree, pear tree, or mango tree, what was the rule? Eat, eat, eat. Devour from it until your belly is content. Try another batch from the other grove in the far corner. Find your favorites and come back to them. Enjoy all the free produce you want while it is still untouched by foreboding weather, insectile infestation, and hazardous chemicals.

While those trees must have been appetizing, there was one uniquely superb tree. For in this garden, God had also planted the tree of life (Gen. 2:9). This tree provided eternal life for these two, and they could eat from it as well. This first family could curb their physical appetites by eating the most exquisitely delicious fruit right off the tree in the Garden of Eden, and they could maintain their eternal standing by eating from the actual produce-bearing, limb-swaying, life-giving tree of life.

Isn't that good? Apparently, it was not good enough. Like Satan, they wanted to be like God and to know what God knows (Gen. 3:5). If they ate from the only forbidden tree, they would possess the power to make an authoritative distinction – what is defined as good. By nibbling on the forbidden fruit, they could make the determination to what they thought was pure and what was evil. They could make the call as to what was right and what was wrong. Apparently, that ability was more enticing and potentially filling than all of the other good trees in the garden and the one tree that allowed them access to eat forever. They chose to gamble on what was forbidden, and they lost all that was permissible.

Tragically, they found out the cost of attempting to rewrite God's definitions. Good is always what God says is good. If you endeavor to revise the manual, you lose access to other gifts. After their sin, the tree of life was now off limits (Gen. 3:22). Attempting to make an acquisition of the definition of goodness took away their purest experiences of goodness.

Why do we assume that God has bad intentions? God is good, and he does good (Ps. 119:68). Everything created by him is good (1 Tim. 4:4). He doesn't desire to withhold any good thing from those walking in goodness (Ps. 84:11). "Every good gift and every perfect gift is from above, coming down from the Father of lights with whom there is no variation or shadow due to change" (Jas. 1:17). God desires for us to experience his goodness, but our skeptical rebellion forces us to miss it so often. The rules that God institutes are never for our pain but for our joy. In an invitation to enjoy more fully all the good that God provides, he commands us to abstain from certain things that will prove to be to our folly.

THE BEAUTY WE NEED

What God has created is good. In fact, it remained good until mankind arrived on the scene. His original intention was that of humanity experiencing unhindered intimacy with the presence of God while eagerly obeying his commands. That reality and opportunity were perfection exemplified. That will be our goodness realized one day. Due to sin, it won't be today, but it is coming. We find the goodness repaired in the person and the work of Jesus. The King went on a rescue mission to reinstate good back into the Kingdom. Jesus would not rest until he made way for us to experience the original intention of God. He went to the tree of death because we rejected the tree of life.

Jesus went to the Garden of Gethsemane to reclaim the goodness lost in the Garden of Eden.

God created a good world, and yet, even marred with sin, there is still good to be found now but an abundant good to be discovered in the life to come. "Oh, taste and see that the LORD is good! Blessed is the man who takes refuge in him!" (Ps. 34:8). The original standard of goodness is yet untouched by our wickedness. Jesus paid the unimaginable price so we could enjoy his initial offer again and walk in his trail-blazing steps behind him. Out of all the delicacies this world offers, there is no feast so delectable as that which the LORD provides within himself!

What God has commanded is good. Even though we want to rebel, God's ways are appropriate ways. His directions are far superior to our leanings. His ways and thoughts are higher and greater and better than ours (Isa. 55:8-9). Since God's ways are right, we should desire for him to teach us his statutes (Ps. 119:68). "He has told you, O man, what is good; and what does the LORD require of you but to do justice, and to love kindness, and to walk humbly with your God?" (Mic. 6:8). He has a clear path. Don't reject his leadings or resent his suggestions. You have walked long enough in what you thought to be correct headings; how well did that destination fare you? How many days have we missed out on promised peace because we doubted that his ways were good (Isa. 48:18)? I beg you to seek the proper ways of the LORD. You can find delight in his commandments, which are incredibly lovely (Ps. 119:47). When you understand that his methods are good, you finally realize that his commandments as no longer burdensome (1 John 5:3).

What God has given is good. Even in our sinful conditions and temporal situations, God still provides beautiful gifts. As humans living in this broken world, shards of his artistry yet breakthrough as common graces given to all. "For he makes his sun rise on the evil and on the good, and sends rain on the just and on the unjust" (Matt. 5:45). The LORD is good to all (Ps. 145:9).

Every sunrise and sunset are opportunities to enjoy his goodness. Each time a rain shower comes, it's an invitation to leave the umbrella at the door and frolic in the deluge with the people nearest and dearest to you. Every passionate kiss from your spouse, every snuggle shared with a blanket-toting child, every delectable meal sensational enough to buckle your knees, every tantalizing book begging you to digest just one more chapter, every soaring soprano stirring you even though you cannot understand the language by which she sings, every current of the gentle creek calming your mind as it skips over the stones, and every other good thing that just arrests your soul and momentarily lifts it from the mundane is evidence yet again that we have an exquisitely good God. The God who delivered free bread from heaven, encouraged intimacy in the Garden, and commanded a day off from work is an exquisite God who has planned very good things for your life.

What God has planned is good. Even amid fear and uncertainty, we can trust that God's goodness will endure. "The LORD is good, a stronghold in the day of trouble; he knows those who take refuge in him" (Nah. 1:7). As difficult times come, he is the good and steady anchor upon which to rely (Heb. 6:19). One of the most quoted verses of the Bible even confirms that God has good plans for us (Jer. 29:11). In that context, God has promised seventy years of exile for the idolatrous ways of his people. As they are preparing to live in that pagan culture for more than a generation, God instructs them to seek the welfare or good of those cities (Jer. 29:7). Even among a godless culture, good could be found. Though they would wait for seventy years to see the promise fulfilled, God had yet a good plan. They just had to wait for it. Eventually, they would see the goodness of the LORD in the land of the living (Ps. 27:13). Through those seasons, they remembered the songs and reminders to "give thanks to the LORD, for he is good, for his steadfast love endures forever!" (Ps. 107:1).

What God has prepared is good. We will skip in the garden again. When Christ returns, all that was made wrong in Eden will be remedied for eternity. "Behold, the dwelling place of God is with man. He will dwell with them, and they will be his people, and God himself will be with them as their God. He will wipe away every tear from their eyes, and death shall be no more, neither shall there be mourning, nor crying, nor pain anymore, for the former things have passed away" (Rev. 21:3-4). Talk about good. We who have made the situation terrible are invited to enter into the presence of the only good one forever, and we are granted access based upon the goodness of another. Instead of making us wallow in the pit we have dug for ourselves, God lifts us up to green pastures yet again.

In heaven, God will transform unacceptable sinners into beautiful saints. It will be unnecessary to clean our feet at the welcome mat of heaven because we will be perfectly pure. On that day, the delicious meals of this world will be forgotten. The beautiful scenery that we snapshot in this life will be humdrum compared to the glories we shall behold. The most significant causes for joy from this planet will no longer be needed, for the most valid source of all joy will be right before us. He has been good, he is good, and oh, your soul is not prepared to see how good he really will be forever.

✂ GOODNESS REVIEW

Incorrect Perception: ~~God is a fuddy-duddy~~.

Correct Attribute: God is good.

Definition: *The goodness of God means that he alone is the filter by which goodness is gauged.*

Focal Verse: *You are good and do good; teach me your statutes (Ps. 119:68).*

Implication: *Our perception of God would change the moment we acknowledge him as the source for all the good in our lives.*

▢ FURTHER STUDY

What concept from this chapter caused you to think differently?

Meditate on James 1:12-18. Why do you think a warning about lusting for what you don't have (Jas. 1:14) is followed by a reminder about acknowledging the good you already have (Jas. 1:17)?

What are some good gifts that the Father gives us?

CORRECTIVE THEOLOGY

Why do you think we have a difficult time believing that God gives good gifts that bring pleasure and joy?

If God is the source of all good things, why is this world full of so many bad things?

If we can find great, yet tainted, joys in this life, what does that imply about the life to come?

CHAPTER 18
THE TALENT JUDGE GOD

The contestant fearfully strolls up to the microphone. Attempting to stay calm and maintain a certain degree of composure only makes her breath quicken more. She couldn't have practiced more for this moment, but she inwardly panics wondering if it was enough. With the bright lights blinding, she can hear the crowd offering generous applause, but she knows that if she fails to deliver, the mercurial support could waiver in a moment.

Positioned in the middle of the room, she sees them. Seated at the table, the professional experts are cautiously awaiting her performance. These talent judges will determine a perspective in moments on a skill that she has taken a lifetime to hone. After a few obligatory questions, one of the judges abruptly commands her to begin. It's now or never. As the music commences, she attempts to give the opportunity the most valiant effort she can possibly muster. In these mere seconds, these judges have the power to start or stop her career. They are unaware she has had a horrible day at work, uncaring she had developed allergies with the changing of the season, and unwilling to wait too long to be wowed. If she is to gain acceptance, she must deliver, and she must deliver now.

Many people's depiction of God is that of a talent judge. As we perform for him, a blasé expression at first gives us no indication regarding how he feels towards us. God is not the loved one on the side believing in us, bragging on us, and encouraging us to share our gift with the world. Instead, we often view God as the harsh critic demanding perfection. Such an expectation scoffs at the notion of a second chance. He is unwilling to exhibit patience with us when we fail to deliver. His ear is magnetized to our wrong notes more than our good ones. Regarding our performance, he would have suggested an alternate song, key, and wardrobe. In fact, his standard is so high, we wouldn't be surprised if he shortened the abbreviated song even more than initially intended and just put us out of our embarrassing misery. With a disapproving grimace, he critiques the entire performance, questions even our attempt in this particular field, and refuses to allow us to advance to the next round. Walking off the stage, our hopeful anticipations fade like the stage lights behind us. We will never earn the respect of this God.

God is not a talent judge. God is love.

THE LOVE OF GOD

The love of God is such a foundational attribute that it creates a unique challenge to describe it. While God is obviously aware of our performance, his standard is so high that no one could possibly meet his expectations. So, how is he in a relationship with any person if none of us can bear the weight of his proper scrutiny? The only reason any of us can know God is because he loves us.

The love of God means God has an unconditional and undeserving affection for us. We struggle accepting an unconditional love in this life. Even if you refuse to admit it, every tenderness we receive on earth has some type of conditions attached to it. The talent judge phenomenon sneaks itself into so many of our personal relationships. The fact of someone's love for us may not be conditional, but the amount of it surely is. Not with God. Since God's character and conditions are so high, there is no way for a person to remain still standing upon the stage. His unconditional affection means he loves us just the way we are. He is not waiting for us to impress him with anything.

God's love is also undeserving. With such impeccable character and worth, it makes no sense to why he would love people as unworthy as us. While his love being unconditional speaks to our inability to exhibit enough positive traits, the undeserving aspect of his passion relates to our ever increasing list of negative qualities. Not only are we deficient in what could make us lovable, but we also excel in what makes us unlovable. Our days are filled with selfish, moody displays of prideful, despicable moments. Our consistent patterns of behavior neglect a needed level of self-awareness. We fail even to acknowledge how broken and busted we are. No wonder we chase people off. Yet God is not frightened by our ugly outbursts. He sees what others see, but he also perceives what no one else does. God is aware of who we are when no one else is around, and yet he still loves us. He beholds what we do, but he can also perceive what we think. Aware of all this incriminating evidence, he somehow still loves us. This undeserving affection is baffling to one who really understands the nature of our unkempt behaviors and chaotic dispositions.

God's love is based on his person and not our performance. That's the only reason why God's love can remain consistent. If it were based upon our performance, his love would change. Since it is based on his person, it is steadfast. His fondness towards us is unmovable and undeterred. The psalmist knew that God's love was so unique that his simple, composed refrain proclaimed, "His steadfast love endures forever" (Ps. 136:1). He understood that God's love was so extreme that he repeated that line twenty-six times in the twenty-six versed song. God's love is so constant that it sounds like a broken record. For every single example of his grace, there is a musical note cascading his endearment towards us.

The definition of love is intrinsically linked with the character of God. "Anyone who does not love does not know God, because God is love" (1 John 4:8). God is the very standard of love. Utilize the equal symbol all you want in this equation. God's nature is the equivalency of love. The only way we can even attempt to love is because we have first been loved by God (1 John 4:19). Our capacity to love one another originates from our reality of being loved by God (1 John 4:7). Every relationship attempting to display a love for another before accepting a love from God is doomed to fail. While there are shreds of evidence of ungodly people demonstrating tender moments, that does not mean that they genuinely understand how to receive or how to give love. A broken clock is right twice a day. People can portray occasional loving actions, but without the image of God ever breaking onto the scene, we are incapable of consistently showing love. God is the definition of love, and all actions that are to be determined as loving or unloving must be filtered by his character. "God is love, and whoever abides in love abides in God, and God abides in him" (1 John 4:16).

This great God, who could justifiably disregard us all, loves unlovable flunkees like ourselves. He doesn't give a fickle love, but he always displays a commitment to an everlasting love (Jer. 31:3). He notably abounds in what is called steadfast love (Ps. 86:15). This type of endearment comes from a different source than what this world boasts of offering. God provides a uniquely, covenant-keeping, abiding love (Deut. 7:9).

While we are undeserving of such love, we must be confident in it. The act of acquiring God's love must always be seen as a reception and not a reward. Since God's love is based upon an unconditional and undeserving framework, we can rest in the fact that his love is the most secure reality in the universe. Since we know relationships so well, we fear that something might eventually hinder our relationship with God. In every other connection, we have experienced severe and trivial issues that have compromised the connection with the other party.

Our enemy knows this very well. He understands the need to interfere with such a life-altering concept as the unconditional, undeserving love of God. So, what is his strategy? He accuses you and me by name before God. Day and night, he calls out to God and exposes our unworthiness (Rev. 12:10). His words are so undeniably accurate that you honestly worry he might legitimately win his case. "He's not worthy! She is so messed up! Do you know what he thinks about? Are you aware of what is in her past? Surely you do not believe that this defendant is worthy of your love, do you God?"

Whether we are eavesdropping on the conversation, Satan is yelling the summarized prosecution in our ears, or we honestly agree with the thorough assessment, we are all too familiar with this devilish, well-informed logic. He is undoubtedly and unfortunately right. We are not worthy of this divine love. But instead of our unworthiness robbing us of God's love, it actually reveals the capacity of how great this love really is. The accused sinners don't have an alibi but do they ever have a witness. "And they have conquered him by the blood of the Lamb and by the word of their testimony" (Rev. 12:11). While Satan's prosecution is robust, Jesus' defense is more exceptional. A plea has been made based on the love of Jesus. He has shed his blood for my soul. Jesus' offering was never based upon an obligation. He wanted to die for us. We overcome the enemy's assessment by his blood and by our testimony. The testimony is this: Jesus loves me. I have an alibi. I have a witness. I can testify that I belong to him. When my crimes were committed, I thought I was away from him, but he never really left me. He stood in my place because of his love for me.

Satan attempts to hinder the connection, but he is hopelessly incapable. Even my sin isn't powerful enough to sever the line. For those thinking that our performances hinder God's love, we have mistaken our ability to dilute something so unwaveringly powerful. Is there anything able to separate us from the love of God? "For I am sure that neither death nor life, nor angels nor rulers, nor things present nor things to come, nor powers, nor height nor depth, nor anything else in all creation, will be able to separate us from the love of God in Christ Jesus our Lord" (Rom. 8:38-39).

God's love for you is consistent because your behavior has always been present before him. When Jesus died on the cross, every single one of your sins was still in the future. There is not a wayward moment that surprised God. When you believe the gospel, you are receiving forgiveness for all past, present, and future sins committed. So when you arrive at a horrible decision, a wayward moment, or a backsliding season, God could see it clearly before it happened and has still chosen to love you.

Not only is God's love for us not contingent upon our performance, but it is motivated by Christ's performance. The cross of Jesus is the proof of God's love. "For God so loved the world, that he gave his only Son, that whoever believes in him should not perish but have eternal life" (John 3:16). God's love is seen through God's gift. When God saw our condition, he gave us the most fabulous gift he could give in his

Son. What love! Jesus reveals his love for us in that he willingly gave himself for us (Gal. 2:20). This type of sacrificial love brings us into the family and reclassifies us as children of God (1 John 3:1). He refused to offer a mediocre affection but offered us a relentless love (Eph. 2:4).

The timing of God's love is paramount to understand. If you get this progression wrong, you get the gospel wrong. "God shows his love for us in that while we were still sinners, Christ died for us" (Rom. 5:8). Jesus died for us *while* we were *still* sinners! If he were after our performance, he would have withheld his love until we were no longer sinners. Since he knew that time would never come, he overtook us with his love while yet we were still filthy. God has never expected someone to clean themselves up to go into his presence. The only cleaner potent enough for such a transformation is the love of God. God's unconditional and undeserving love is the only force powerful enough to clean up sinners like me.

THE ACCEPTANCE WE NEED

God's love precedes our worth. His love is actually what provides our value. He will not withhold his affection while he waits on you to earn it. God loves you right now. He even likes you right now. God does not offer an unaffectionate devotion with a resentful disposition. His love is forever an eager infatuation.

God has never loved you more than he does right now, and God could never love you more than he does right now.

God doesn't love the next version of yourself. He adores the current model. While Jesus is the perfect Son of God, the Father's heart is revealed at his baptism as he bellows from the heavens, "You are my beloved Son; with you I am well pleased" (Luke 3:22). Before it was ever recorded that Jesus preached a sermon, befriended a sinner, or addressed a need, God loved him. God's love wasn't based upon Jesus' ministry track record, and it is no different from his love for you. He is not waiting for you to provide a catalyst for his love.

18: THE TALENT JUDGE GOD

When my daughter was a toddler, she was a stuffed animal hoarder. The more she received, the more she wanted, and she had enough family members and friends who were eager to supply her with an unending arsenal of pink fluffiness. Some nights I would check on her sleeping only to have to dig through furry friends just to make sure she was still in there. Despite all the expensive and fancy stuffed animals that she has been given, she had an inseparable favorite. Violet the Wolf went with her everywhere. This tiny varmint was clothed with pink and purple. Violet wasn't the most elaborate or the most expensive, but it was her absolute favorite. Among all the other animals and dolls, Violet was her consistent companion. That's what made the tragedy all the more critical. I was alerted at work one day that Violet had gone missing. Unsure of her whereabouts, my daughter was inconsolable. Distracting her with another toy did not work. Committing to buy a replacement did not suffice. She wanted Violet, and she could not rest until she was reunited with Violet.

As I retraced her steps through parking lots, van seats, and visited locations, I almost quit. I thought the search was hopeless. Much to my surprise, I finally found the tiny wolf. Nestled among other items in a lost-and-found, Violet stared at me as if she wondered what took me that long. The doll on her left was more expensive. The toy on her right had more impressive features. But among items of higher quality, Violet had superior worth. She was not superior due to her quality but the quality of the one who loved her.

If you have ever felt as if you are not worthy of the love of God, I can relate. I realize that I don't possess a worth that deserves love, yet my worth comes from the fact that I am loved by God. My value comes not from my quality but by the quality of the one who loves me. God loves me with an unrelenting and unashamed love. Do you struggle with insecurity? Your heart will find its remedy in the center of God's love. "The LORD your God is in your midst, a mighty one who will save; he will rejoice over you with gladness; he will quiet you by his love; he will exult over you with loud singing" (Zeph. 3:17). With rowdy serenading and boisterous dancing, God quiets my anxious soul by proving to be the giddy Father who loves me just the way I am. He isn't dancing because of anticipation of who you will become but due to an acknowledgment of who you already are.

✂ LOVE REVIEW

Incorrect Perception: ~~God is a talent judge~~.

Correct Attribute: *God is love.*

Definition: *The love of God means he has an unconditional and undeserving affection for us.*

Focal Verse: *But God shows his love for us in that while we were still sinners, Christ died for us (Rom. 5:8).*

Implication: *God's love for me is not contingent upon my performance for him.*

▯ FURTHER STUDY

What idea from this chapter emboldened your affections for God?

Meditate on Zephaniah 3:14-20. What do you notice about God's commitment to his people?

How does the description of God's love in Zephaniah 3:17 challenge our common perceptions of him?

CORRECTIVE THEOLOGY

What are the pieces of evidence that reveal that even religious people expect God's love to vary by the degree of our individual worth?

Why do you find it difficult to accept that God has a jovial, committed love for you?

What would change in your life if you genuinely believed that God loves you as much as the Bible says he does?

CHAPTER 19
THE CHUTES & LADDERS GOD

Chutes and Ladders is a game that seeks to reach the top of the board before other opponents do. While the spinner determines how many blocks you advance for each turn, specific squares teach the players a moral lesson. You move higher by climbing ladders when you perform good deeds, but you slide lower on the chutes when you break the rules. Any varying level of success or failure can change in a moment with a simple action. The lesson it teaches children is that you climb higher faster by the more helpful handouts that you give and fall further into oblivion for all the dastardly deeds you do.

Many people follow the Chutes and Ladders God. This syncretistic version of God attempts to infuse the God of the Bible with the philosophy of karma. Karma is the belief that if you do good, you will receive good. If you do bad, you will receive bad. In our culture, many people may deny a religious belief in karma, but they adhere to it practically. We all enjoy when someone gets what they deserve as long as that someone isn't us. Believing God to reward moral behavior and to discipline immoral behavior, we reckon that God is dependent upon our ethical integrity to determine how he should best deal with us. The danger of such a belief is assuming that anyone is worthy of God's love and conjecturing that anyone is beyond God's love.

This concept is so full of landmines. Of course, doing good is a far superior route than doing evil. When given a chance for obedience or disobedience, always choose obedience. Yet while we strive for such dedication, we must realize that none are ever so obedient enough to warrant God's approval. God's love for us is not contingent upon our devotion to him. You cannot do enough good deeds to climb the ladders into God's presence. You cannot do enough evil actions to plummet you to a depth from which God cannot reach. There has never been a ladder high enough or a chute low enough to reposition ourselves in the presence of God. No person has ever been too high or too low for God to reach him or her. While God is aware of records, he is not hindered because of them. If we can reconnect with God, it will be because he crosses the chasm and not because we figured out how to alleviate the distance.

God does not operate like a Chutes and Ladders board game. God is gracious.

THE GRACE OF GOD

The grace of God is foundational for our salvation and our sanctification. Without the grace of God, we have absolutely no basis for a relationship with him. As rebels who have defied the King of kings, we are morally unfit to remain within the Kingdom. The only way we can regain citizenship is if the King does something remarkable to open up the gates to us again. Our only hope for solace is if he provides it. We are utterly dependent upon the grace of God.

The grace of God is the unmerited, unwarranted, and undeserved favor of God towards unrighteous sinners. It is imperative that we unpack this definition of grace. We use words like grace, mercy, love, and favor interchangeably, and yet there are significant differences. The mercy of God means that we do not receive what we deserve. The grace of God means that we receive what we do not deserve. We are grateful for what mercy spares us and for what grace gives us.

God's grace is an undeserved gift. Anything that you think is warranted to you for your behavior is not a gift. We don't deserve God's love; we are granted God's love. According to Scripture, the only thing that we deserve is death (Rom. 6:23), hell (Rev. 21:8), and wrath (Rom. 1:18). So if we receive anything less than that, it is only by the mercy of God. You never want to seek procurement of what you deserve from God.

The grace of God is greater than our sin. "Where sin increased, grace abounded all the more" (Rom. 5:20). What unexpected grace that is able to cover such unmeasurable sin! My sin is rampant, but if we attempt to quantify the summation of humanity's sin throughout history, the number still falls short of God's grace. God is more committed to his grace than you are addicted to your vice. God is more thorough with his grace than you are determined to have your way. God is more obsessed in offering grace than you are bent on escaping punishment. Add up all the transgressions from the toddlers to the Hitlers, multiply them to the nth degree, and he still miraculously gives greater grace.

The grace of God is a fantastic offering that can never be based upon obligation. We cannot blackmail God into obtaining grace. We are unable to even acquire a legitimate bargaining chip. If we receive grace, it is only because he desired to give it to us. He is gracious to whom he wants to be gracious (Exod. 33:19). If it isn't his decision, that means it is based on works instead of grace. Our best attempts at righteousness are nothing but filthy rags before him (Isa. 64:6). He gives grace willingly, not begrudgingly. Where he bestows favor, it is never based upon obligation. Grace must be a gift of a love so surprising, or else it is a salary for a job well done.

The grace of God is often spoken of in the Bible as the favor of God. When Noah was selected to be the ark's builder and captain, he obtained this position because he "found favor in the eyes of the LORD" (Gen. 6:8). God graced him with that opportunity. While Scripture claims that Noah was holy, he was still in need of grace. "Noah was a righteous man, blameless in his generation. Noah walked with God" (Gen. 6:9). Notice that grace preceded righteousness in these verses. Noah found grace and performed righteousness. Yet even in his obedience, he was not perfect. Being morally superior to the people of his day was not that difficult of a task, but he also proved that he wasn't blameless. He became so drunk after the flood that he streaked naked ashamedly in front of his family (Gen. 9:21). Good thing he had received God's grace, because, even by being the most righteous man at that time, he was not honorable enough to warrant an extension of a relationship with God based on merit.

As Moses sought God's presence for the continuation of his journey, he experienced God's grace. God replied, "This very thing that you have spoken I will do, for you have found favor in my sight, and I know you by name" (Exod. 33:17). Was Moses righteous? If you compared Moses to the deplorable Egyptians or the idolatrous Israelites, he was at least ethical. If you compared him to the Great I AM, he was in serious trouble. God's willingness to go with Moses was based upon God's unmerited favor rather than Moses' hopeful reward.

Salvation has never come at any time by any means other than grace. "For by grace you have been saved through faith. And this is not your own doing; it is the gift of God, not a result of works, so that no one may boast" (Eph. 2:8-9). A system acquiring salvation through works would have caused a competitive religion full of prideful boasters instead of a grateful family full of humble recipients.

Salvation is and always will be a gift of a gracious God and not a paycheck for upright behavior.

If you think you have earned salvation, you have not received it. Salvation is not your own doing. It is always an unmerited gift from God. Grace has never been offered outside the person and work of Jesus. Many people falsely claim that the Law provided the way for Old Testament figures into heaven, and grace got the New Testament individuals into heaven. The gracious, willing cross of Jesus is the only way anyone gets into heaven regardless of their timeframe.

Even when Jesus was unnamed and unknown, his grace was the sole means of salvation. As the prophets pointed to the coming Messiah, they placed their faith in God's promised deliverance even though they couldn't see all the details clearly (1 Pet. 1:10-12). Even though the gospel had not yet been fully articulated, the faith in the sacrificial system pointing to Jesus was the means of salvation. It was grace through faith. Even Abraham's faith was by grace. God blessed this unlikely man and promised that someone would come from his family to bless all the nations of the earth (Gen. 12:3). As Abraham believed in that promise, God credited righteousness to his account (Gen. 15:6). How could a weak coward who would rather his wife endure shame rather than himself experience mistreatment be called righteous? It can only be because righteousness is a gift instead of a trophy. As he looked forward to a future Messiah coming from his bloodline, he trusted God at his Word, and his salvation was confirmed through an unknown and unclear impending gracious sacrifice.

This favor of God is so glorious that the devil has concocted numerous combatants to war against its establishment within our souls. These opposing philosophies have ruined many people. The three most dangerous enemies to grace are legalism, antinomianism, and maturism.

Legalism is the belief that prioritizes the keeping of the Law by neglecting the power of God's grace. By adhering to a strict list of rules, the legalist believes he or she can earn the favor of God. Salvation by grace is the exact opposite of salvation by human merit (Rom. 3:23-24). People who believe you must clean your act up before coming to God fail to realize that his standard is too immaculate to approach. If a holy prerequisite were required for a relationship with God, none of us would ever be able to access him.

Antinomianism is the belief that believers are no longer held to commandment expectations due to the grace of God. It is a position of having "no law." The Law was first given to a people who had already been redeemed. Commandments were never provided as a hurdle to jump in order to escape slavery, but they were presented as a standard to those who had been rescued from slavery. For those who believe we no longer have to keep the Law, they desire a moral levity that condones sinful behavior. The danger in this belief leads to a moral decline that cheapens God's grace. For believers, the grace of Jesus should crucify ourselves to the world (Gal. 6:14) and cause us to hate sin (Rom. 6:1-2). Why would we want to cuddle up to the transgressions that placed Jesus upon the cross?

Maturism is the belief that no further development is necessary. Some people believe that the grace of God saves but unfortunately neglect that it is also that which sustains. Grace is the foundation for the daily

Christian life. "By the grace of God I am what I am, and his grace toward me was not in vain. On the contrary, I worked harder than any of them, though it was not I, but the grace of God that is with me" (1 Cor. 15:10). You have not matured to a level that exempts you from the need of God's continual grace and progressive growth.

THE OPPORTUNITY WE NEED

Grace provides the opportunity for second chances. Grace is only given to those who acknowledge their sin (1 John 1:9). If you claim a type of moral perfection that sees grace as unnecessary, you are insinuating that Christ died in vain. If we could work our way to heaven, then Jesus' death is barbaric senselessness. Why would Christ die on earth if you could earn a seat in heaven? You will arrive on judgment day either touting your moral scorecard or God's unwarranted grace. If you feel as if you don't need his grace, you will realize at that moment that you needed it more than you could possibly imagine.

Grace is given to those while still in sin. You cannot clean your act up. Be thankful that God didn't wait on us to improve. "God shows his love for us in that while we were still sinners, Christ died for us" (Rom. 5:8). Jesus died for us *while* we were sinners, not *after* we were sinners. Jesus was graciously offering salvation to the crowd while they were still shouting for his crucifixion (Luke 23:34). Our sins must be seen in the light of that history. All of our sins were in the future when he died on the cross! There is no sin committed for an additional time that removes his desire to canvas us with grace.

Grace is given to those who have nothing left to give. When you get to the end of your rope and realize that you have nothing to offer God, you are finally ready to receive something from God. The prodigal son (Luke 15:11-32) desired his father's inheritance more than his father's presence. He squandered it away on loose living and cheap pursuits. When he came to his senses as he longed to eat the pods from the pigs he was paid to feed, he decided to go home to be a servant in his father's house. He had lost the opportunity to be a son, but at least he could still be a servant. The income and conditions would be far better there than what he was experiencing at that moment.

"He arose and came to his father. But while he was still a long way off, his father saw him and felt compassion, and ran and embraced him and kissed him" (Luke 15:20). With nothing left to offer, exchange, or repay, his father welcomed him back. Refusing to give him a job as a slave, he embraced him again as a son. All that the son had taken from his father had been spent in sinful obsessions. It was gone. It wasn't coming back. Nevertheless, the father's love had never wavered. With nothing left to give his father, the son still received. Somehow the father still had enough in the account to pamper his son with an unforgettable party that surpassed all the ones he had forgotten about. It's grace. It's not works.

We have often spoken about reaching heaven's gates. Culture has added much extra-biblical material to the imagination. Since Peter is commonly referred to as the gatekeeper, the stories usually go that he will ask us why he should let us into heaven. As a youngster, I remember preachers telling me that heaven was going to have a particular room where God played a video of your life. One version would be a replay, but he would also show another variant that could have been a reality if I had been more obedient. In those videos, I would probably see more chutes than I would ladders.

Scripture teaches that Christ covers our sins completely. Jesus paid it all. He didn't have to put our sin debt on a credit card while being forced to make monthly payments because his credit was low. We don't have to assist his payment plan either – the debt is gone! I will not enter heaven to be immediately placed upon trial for my transgressions because Christ has already dealt with them in full. Any squabbling attempts at excuses for my lackluster effort on earth will be foreign there. "God, I am so sorry about all that sin I committed down there. I know there's supposedly a video and such, and I know that you probably feel like putting me in heaven's timeout for a millennium or two. I really do regret all this sin that I brought with me."

God has only one response on that day: "What sin? It wasn't allowed beyond the gates. That was taken care of a long time ago. Well done, my good and faithful servant." What have I done to receive such a welcome? Nothing. If I get what I deserve, I will never enter heaven or behold Jesus, yet that will not be my story. What unthinkable grace.

✂ **GRACE** REVIEW

Incorrect Perception: ~~God operates like a Chutes & Ladders board game~~.

Correct Attribute: *God is gracious.*

Definition: *The grace of God is the unmerited, unwarranted, and undeserved favor of God towards unrighteous sinners.*

Focal Verse: *But if it is by grace, it is no longer on the basis of works; otherwise grace would no longer be grace (Rom. 11:6).*

Implication: *God's grace is even greater than my sin.*

🗔 **FURTHER** STUDY

What specific thought from this chapter encouraged you?

Meditate on Ephesians 2:1-10. Based on this passage, what makes God's grace so amazing?

If you were to explain grace to another using Ephesians 2:8-9, how would you best describe it?

CORRECTIVE THEOLOGY

Out of legalism, antinomianism, or maturism, which is your most dangerous tendency?

Why is grace such a complicated truth to accept in our society?

If someone asked you why you would get to enter heaven, what would your response be?

CHAPTER 20
THE BUFFET GOD

Buffet lines have much to teach us regarding our selective appetites. While the rise of restaurants over the years have increased our quest for options, the invention of buffets has even multiplied our picky tendencies and our indulgent cravings. As you survey through the numerous choices, you select what appeals to you and ignore what disinterests you. Picking and choosing what to pile on your plate makes you the definitive filter by which all morsels must be judged. Your meal is entirely unique to you. No other plate will look precisely like yours. Ultimately, that is the goal. With the freedom to choose, you can feast upon what you desire and neglect what you would rather not have to stomach.

We often approach God as if he functions like a buffet. In embracing a Wiki God mentality, we seek to serve a deity who has traits by which we can sift. While there are plenty of options before us, we will ultimately determine what the finished product looks like. Our dubious approach places God upon a theological buffet in which we pick and choose those delicacies in which we enjoy and pass over the dishes upon which we would rather not chew. If a doctrine seems advantageously palatable for me, I will gladly scarf it down and return for seconds. If some concept seems too foreign or too difficult to digest, I leave it upon the line expecting someone else to pick it up. Going down the line with my tray in hand, I am the grand determiner of what the God platter looks like in my life. My appetite for him originates not from the feast he prepared but the menu of which I created.

God is not a buffet line. God is God.

THE PERFECTION OF GOD

In the opening pages of this volume, I expressed the need for a biblical theology over a personal philosophy. Instead of making God behave like you think he should, it is far superior to embrace God as he really is. Our versions of God could never compete with his own personal identity. He knows what he should be like far better than our hypothesized theories or hopeful ideations. God is utterly perfect. He is exactly who he should be because no one could ever concoct a superior version than who he consistently remains to be.

Accepting ancient beliefs does not mean you hold antiquated values. If there is a God, he does not need to improve his thoughts or catch up with the times. If he has plans, they do not need to adjust. If he has provided the truth, we do not need to submit a revision. Eternal truths have contemporary significance. "Remember the former things of old; for I am God, and there is no other; I am God, and there is none like me" (Isa 46:9). We do not need another version of God. There is none like him, and that is a good thing.

We shouldn't strive to imitate Adam and Eve's rebellion to know what God knows (Gen. 3:6). When will we see the futility of Aaron's error of carving gods (Exod. 32:4) out of the gifts that the true God gives us (Exod. 12:35-36)? Protect us from the tendency to worship God in the tabernacle while having an idol in the satchel (Josh. 24:14). Help us flee from the example of Israel when they sought to replace the omnipotent God with an earthly king of impressive physical stature (1 Sam. 8:5; 9:2; 10:23) yet lacking brave leadership acumen (1 Sam. 10:22; 17:11). We should be cognizant of the fact that religious scholars eagerly looking for the Messiah met him face to face and put him on a cross (Mark 15:31-32). In all our expectations of what God should be, we are in danger of missing him altogether.

In a culture that desires amended values and updated allowances, the truth about God is capable of enduring. Since his character and conduct are perfect, they need not change with the times. In a definitive study of God, we find the perfect one who needs no alterations. Any adjustments made to him would disfigure the ideal face for which our souls ultimately long to behold.

20: THE BUFFET GOD

What makes us so quick to desert biblical theology and so eager to defend personal beliefs? The Apostle Paul wrote, "I am astonished you are so quickly deserting him who called you in the grace of Christ and are turning to a different gospel" (Gal. 1:6). Out of concern for a church who was altering the message of the gospel, he understood that they were ultimately trying to recreate the identity of God. These dangerous members desired to trouble others by distorting the gospel of Christ (Gal. 1:7). This struggle is not unique to the churches in Galatia. Churches throughout history have endured through countless conflicts on the same topic. In addition, many people in our day are turning away from a biblical gospel and denying the biblical attributes of God. What will we do? Will we give way to political and peer pressure, or will we seek to stand firm on an authority that has a longer shelf life than a meager couple of years?

In our current cultural climate, I am regularly tempted to cut pieces of biblical truth from my worldview in order to be widely accepted. I struggle with copying some popular dogma to utilize myself. In a desire to avoid tension, I ponder if pasting some outlook into my beliefs will increase others' consent of me. Cut, copy, and paste. Among all my attempted edits upon God, I end up looking at a portrayal that no longer looks like God.

For all the divergent adjustments I endeavor to make, I end up beholding not a picture of God but a reflection of me. The effort of holding up a mirror would have been so much more straightforward than all the edits I labored to make. Taking a step back for a thorough glance, I am shocked by what I see. The image is no longer terrifyingly glorious; it is glaringly repulsive. This alteration is the tragically overlooked differentiation between the first two commands. The first commandment is about worshiping the correct God (Exod. 20:2); the second commandment is about worshiping God in the correct way (Exod. 20:3). Don't look at another god versus making him look like another god. When we attempt to edit God, we break the second commandment.

In my longing to appease my appetites and to achieve others' acceptance, I have tried to recreate God in my image. Paul's following declaration to those Galatian believers ring true for us today: "For am I now seeking the approval of man, or of God? Or am I trying to please man? If I were still trying to please man, I would not be a servant of Christ" (Gal. 1:10). We can please man, or we can please God, but it is doubtful if we can do both.

If God's Word is true, the pursuit of this life's acceptance will be short-lived and less than awe-inspiring. If I can endure the criticism for a few decades, I will be able to enjoy the glory for an endless eternity. Jesus even warned us, "Whoever denies me before men, I also will deny before my Father who is in heaven" (Matt. 10:33). Denying the identity of God will lead to a removal from the presence of God. It only makes sense that would happen since our lifelong attempts have been focused on altering his identity in the first place. We must embrace who God is now in order to embrace him forever.

To be received by the Christ, you will be rejected by the culture. "For the word of the cross is folly to those who are perishing, but to us who are being saved, it is the power of God" (1 Cor. 1:18). For those freehand drawing their own image of God, the biblical depiction will appear ridiculous. Those perishing will scoff at the true God all the while cuddling up to their god who will be unable to save them in the end. For those receiving the gospel and accepting God as he is, even persecution is soberly welcomed because it is proof of our alignment with him (2 Tim. 3:12; 1 John 3:1).

Even if you seek to adhere to a biblical worldview, you might be in danger of developing a hybrid doctrinal stance. Maybe you hold to most of the tenants of Christianity, but you try to ignore the ones that complicate your snug theological system. If you have a chapter of Scripture or a book of the Bible that you avoid studying because it challenges, unsettles, or disagrees with you, your actions imply that your ideas are superior to God's truth. Your efforts reveal that you think the biblical portrayal of God is insufficient, and you think you can fix it. God doesn't have a bad side. He doesn't need repositioning in your light.

Don't settle for your version of God. I promise that he is better than you can imagine him to be. Not only is his identity sufficient, but his activity is impeccable. When the Bible disagrees with your beliefs, I can guarantee who is in the wrong. In light of those moments where your eyes are opened, and your head is aching, don't avoid wrestling through the complex truths of God. As you plunge into those depths, never neglect the simple truths at the surface from which we will never escape. You will never graduate from the gospel.

Don't bend the Scriptures if they seem to break your system. Embrace who God is rather than who you want him to be. If you have to perform systematic backflips to make Scripture fit within your theological system, your doctrine is weak and unreliable. Don't make Scripture fit your system; allow Scripture to determine your system. Beware of theological camps that seek to divide the Body of Christ by espousing their prideful positions on doctrinal complexities. Never major in the minors or attempt to make the non-essentials essential.

As you study and share theology, let humility reign. If you are studying Christ more, you should be exhibiting further Christlikeness. If pride is the hallmark of your theology, some essential component is lacking. As believers, we are called to have a defense always ready to share, but we should share it with gentleness and respect (1 Pet. 3:15).

Whether you are interacting with a lost person or a misguided Christian, your demeanor should be helpful rather than harmful. "Have nothing to do with foolish, ignorant controversies; you know that they breed quarrels. And the Lord's servant must not be quarrelsome but kind to everyone, able to teach, patiently enduring evil, correcting his opponents with gentleness. God may perhaps grant them repentance leading to a knowledge of the truth, and they may come to their senses and escape from the snare of the devil, after being captured by him to do his will" (2 Tim. 2:23-26). What a great exhortation for us all to heed. In another's quest for truth, let us pray that we are never a hindrance.

The message of the Bible is sufficient. God's plan for redemption through the ages is more than adequate even if it confuses and shocks the masses. The cross is foolishness (1 Cor. 1:18). The cross is offensive (Gal. 5:11). Yet at the cross, we find all of God's attributes beautifully aligned. While rejected by many, those who receive the gospel will be able to perceive all of who God is while beholding Jesus at the foot of the cross.

- In his *independence*, we see that God needed no other's assistance to bring about salvation.

- In his *transcendence*, we behold a God who has orchestrated every single redemptive detail.

- In his *immanence*, we gasp at the fact that God came so near to take our punishment away.

- In his *eternality*, we recognize the grand plan that God has been weaving together, which culminated at the cross.

- In his *immutability*, we realize that God is unwilling to change his demands for justice or his commitment to grace.

- In his *omnipotence*, we watch at how the curtain tears in two with invisible hands ripping it apart to provide access yet again to the presence of God.

- In his *omnipresence*, we understand how he simultaneously enlightened the onlooking soldier, mesmerized the anxious authorities, and comforted the distressed disciples.

- In his *omniscience*, we see how he placed prophecies in motion that could not be intentionally fulfilled unless this crucifixion was designed by God.

- In his *wisdom*, we stand in awe at how he was willing to allow an unspeakable tragedy to continue in order to secure an unbelievable redemption.

- In his *sovereignty*, we study how he seemed to be somehow in charge of his own death even while shackled and surrounded.

- In his *faithfulness*, we marvel at how he determinately endured through the horror of the cross accompanied by unbridled joy.

- In his *holiness*, we fall down in reverence at the sight of the now unveiled Holy of Holies.

- In his *righteousness*, we stand in awe of his perfect life which never exhibited a single moment of rebellion.

- In his *justice*, we tremble at the terrible consequences of our sin.

- In his *mercy*, we shudder at how God is willing to withhold what we deserve because Jesus stood in wrath's way.

- In his *goodness*, we delight that the greatest reward that the cross provides is reconciliation with God himself.

- In his *love*, we are unable to come up with valid reasoning for why God would set his unrivaled affection upon rebels like us.

- In his *grace*, we find freedom so astounding and forgiveness yet so complete.

The cross provides the opportunity to know God again.

The cross is more than a means of salvation from something. The cross saves us for something. Not only are you saved from enduring God's punishment, but you are saved to experience God's presence. If you view Jesus as a ticket into heaven rather than the treasure of heaven, your motives need to be evaluated. What you consider to be salvation just might be prosperity. Jesus should be the obsession of this life and not just the avenue for a heavenly retirement in the next life. You will love the streets of gold, but you will adore the one who laid the path more.

God is perfect. Don't attempt to change a single thing about him. He is everything we have ever needed and nothing like what we ever expected. Praise the Lord for such a surprising development. God is not turning out to be who I thought he should be, and how my soul is ever relieved at each new realization of that truth.

THE GOD WE NEED

The God of the Bible may not be who I wanted, but he is who I needed. With each step closer to knowing him, I discover that my previous ideas pale in comparison to his actual identity. Not only do I understand that I was wrong, but I find joy in being saved from my former ignorance. He is far better than I could have even imagined. Nothing is impossible for my God.

In the beginning, God was there. There was nothing before him, and there is no one like him. He created this universe and absolutely everything in it. When he said, "let there be light," the light had no choice but to obey. He had not yet created a sun or moon yet. With even no stars above, he simply spoke light into existence, and the darkness was overcome. He didn't need the light for he was the light.

My God created the heavens and the earth. All that we see, know, and experience he made in seven days. Every year, leading scientists discover a constellation never seen before, and my God in heaven replies, "Are you just now getting to that one? You think that is impressive. You ain't seen nothing yet. Keep on coming." Every constellation and every creature, every bit of scenery and every change of season, everything from the east to the west was made by his power and for his glory. God steps back at his Creation and calls it good, but Creation steps back and looks at my God and calls him great. You know why? Because nothing is impossible for my God.

My God was able to breathe the breath of life into dust and make mankind. He created you. He created me. He didn't create us because he was lonely or needy; he created us for his glory. We were made by him, and we were made for him.

My God was able to change a barren void into a vibrant Creation. My God was able to transform a childless home into a burgeoning nation.

20: THE BUFFET GOD

My God was able to redeem an enslaved people. He rescued his own from the clutches of a mighty Pharaoh and sunk the world's most feared army under the waters of the Red Sea. My God took over management of the Promised Land and gave it to a caravan unable to procure victory by their own strength.

My God was able to take ordinary people and make them accomplish extraordinary things. He brought down walls with the sound of trumpets. He scattered armies by the shouts of priests. He brought down significant giants by the hands of insignificant shepherds. He sent kings shaking with the waving of his hand, and yet he still humbles the mightiest in this world by the mere mentioning of his name. You know why? Because nothing is impossible for my God.

My God could take the voices of lone prophets and bring nations to their knees. He led the lone prophet Elijah to defeat hundreds of idolatrous priests in a holy battle of pyromania. He led the exiled prophet Daniel to confront the most powerful king in the world until he was groveling upon his knees. He led the runaway prophet Jonah to be vomited by a giant fish to speak a simple message to a godless nation and watch them wailing on the ground in repentance. You know why? Because nothing is impossible for my God.

My God is unwavering. No matter the depth of our sin, he continued to love. No matter our treatment of each other, he continued to pursue. No matter the severity of our crimes, he provided a second chance.

We could not make it to him, and so he came to us. Immanuel, God with us. Jesus Christ, God in the flesh, dwelt among us, and we could never be the same. Who can speak all things into existence? Who can make saints out of misfits? Who can restore peace from our strife? Whose power can bring the dead back to life? His name is Jesus. Only Jesus.

He is the Christ - the Son of the Living God. The Long-Awaited Messiah of whom all history was longing for finally appeared and the world has yet to recover. He came to love the unlovable, reach the unreachable, and forgive the unforgivable. He healed the sick, cleansed the lepers, and befriended the sinners. The mute could speak, the deaf could hear, the lame could walk, and now the blind can truly see.

And yes, my Jesus died, but nobody took advantage of him. He wasn't forced upon that cross. He made that cross. He volunteered for that cross. He came eagerly looking for that cross. And while he may have died upon that cross, he was never defeated upon that cross. Joy brought him there, and grace would keep him there. Our sins were great, but his grace was greater. The wrath of God meant for us was placed upon him at that cross. It was not because any rebellious man or governing authority or devil of hell put him there, but because he desired to go there.

He took our unrighteousness. He offered his own righteousness. For our sake, he who knew no sin became sin so that in him, we might become the righteousness of God. The wrath of God was heading our way, and Jesus stepped into our place. He took the death that I should have died so that now I can live the life that he has lived. He is the way. He is the truth. He is the life, and yet he was willing to give his up so we could have ours back.

But church, lest you forget, let me remind you that the cross was not the end. While his enemies were rejoicing, the authorities celebrating, his followers regrouping, his disciples doubting, and those women crying, my Jesus was busy rising. No cross could defeat him. No government could pacify him. No demonic force could control him. No sin could keep him. No grave could contain him. No death could restrain him. He got up. How could it be? Because nothing is impossible for my God.

Sin was defeated. Satan was disarmed. Hell lost its sting. Death misplaced its victory.

There was nothing before him; there will be nothing after him. There is nothing like him. He had no predecessor. He will have no successor. He is the author and the finisher. He is the Alpha and the Omega. He is the beginning and last, future and past, there has never been a moment when he was not, and there will never be a moment that he will not be.

My God still reigns supreme. No matter who is president or candidate, he is still the King of kings and the Lord of lords. No Supreme court governs him. No senate or house revokes him. No cabinet advises him. No secret service guards him. No lobbyist sways him. He says what he wants, and he does what he wants.

My God is unstoppable. Nations try to restrict him. Rulers try to avoid him. Dictators try to sway him. Governments try to ignore him. But he cannot be contained, maintained, or restrained. He cannot be shut up, backed up, or held up. No power can keep his influence out. No opposition can keep his message quiet, and no authority can hinder his plans from going forth.

The more they try to restrict this King, the more they see his Kingdom coming. The more they try to threaten his children, the more they see his love spreading. The more they try to keep him out, the more they see his presence invading.

My God is sufficient. He doesn't need a handout or a bailout. He is not short on resources or manpower.

My God is all-wise. Diseases in which doctors have closed the book, my God writes a new chapter. Marriages in which counselors have to refer, my God lifts them from the ashes. Homes which are broken, he restores. Those deep in need, he provides all the more. Broken, weary, depressed, and confused, my God can bring life anew. Do you know why? Because nothing is impossible for my God.

He is mighty, magnificent, and majestic. Omniscient and omnipresent. Immanent and transcendent. Immutable, irrefutable, unstoppable, unforgettable. Good, just, right, and holy, powerful, supreme, my one and only. He can do anything. He is my everything. He is the sinless Savior, the righteous Redeemer, the Mighty God and the truest friend, the King of kings and the Lord of lords; he is the Son of God and the Son of Man. Who is this warrior who secured victory? Who is this truth setting us free? Who is this sacrifice able to save us? There is no other - only Jesus.

Angels fall on their faces. Demons fall to their knees. And there is still coming a day on which every knee will bow, and every tongue will confess that Jesus Christ is Lord. He's not through with me, and I cannot get over him.

My God is able to finish what he started. And when he comes back, he ain't coming to take sides; he's coming to take over. With a mighty shout, in a split second, all that once was wrong will be made right again. And when that trumpet sounds and he splits the skies, he will crush the enemy once and for all, and will call out to his children and finally beckon us to "come back home."

Rise up, church, for I have good news for you today. No matter what chapter you are reading right now, I have read the end of the book, and guess what? We win. We win. We win. No more tears, no more pain, no more death, no more sin, no more enemy; only Jesus, Jesus, and more of Jesus. We win. We win. We win.

You know why? Because nothing is impossible for my God. That's the mighty God that I serve. Is that the God that you serve?

✂ PERFECTION REVIEW

Incorrect Perception: ~~We should treat God as a buffet.~~

Correct Belief: *God is God.*

Focal Verse: *Remember the former things of old; for I am God, and there is no other; I am God, and there is none like me (Isa. 46:9).*

Implication: *If God is not turning out to be who you thought he should be, that should be seen as a welcomed discovery in your life.*

📄 FURTHER STUDY

What specific concept from this chapter stretched you?

Meditate on Matthew 10:16-33. How did Jesus warn his disciples regarding being faithful witnesses in a rebellious culture?

Based on Matthew 10:32-33, how is portraying a biblical theology essential both now and later?

 CORRECTIVE THEOLOGY

Out of all the attributes mentioned, what is the one that you speak of the most often? What does that reveal about you?

Out of all the attributes mentioned, what is the one that still challenges you the greatest? What does that reveal about you?

What are some practical steps you can take to ensure you continue to develop in your understanding of the biblical attributes of God?

SCRIPTURE INDEX

Genesis
1:1   23, 53
1:2   43
1:26-27   166
1:31   83, 173
2:1   83
2:7   43
2:9   57, 174
2:16-17   173
2:17   104, 152
3:5   8, 174
3:6   202
3:8   43, 85
3:9   85
3:22   174
3:24   44
6:6   66.
6:8   193
6:9   193
7:16   44
9:21   193
11:1-9   38
12:3   27, 195
15:6   195
18:1   44
18:14   74
18:25   153
18:27   35
21:33   24, 53
28:15   123
28:16   86
28:17   35
32:30   44
32:31   35
39:2   44, 143
39:3   44
39:21   44
39:23   45
49:10   143
50:15-21   148
50:20   143

Exodus
3:5   134
3:6   134
3:12   44
3:14   25
4:12   45
12:35-36   202
14:27   133
15:11   132
20:2   203
20:3   203
20:16   123
21:32   166
32:4   202
32:9-14   66
32:10   67
32:32   66
33:11   44
33:17   194
33:19   193
34:6   163

Leviticus
18:4   154

Numbers
23:19   64, 123, 123, 133

Deuteronomy
1:30-31   43, 87
4:6-8   107
4:7   46
4:31   163
4:39   43
7:9   184
10:14   85
10:17-18   155
29:29   105, 117
30:15   113
31:8   86
32:4   153, 158
32:39   116
34:10   44

Joshua
1:5   44, 45
1:9   44, 86
5:14   134
5:15   134, 135
6:17   143
6:20   133
6:27   44
7:1   143
24:14   143, 202

Judges
7:19   133
21:25   144

1 Samuel
2:2   138
3:19   44

7:12	127	38:4	23
8:5	202	38:35	162
8:18	66	40:4	35, 46
9:2	202	40:9	162
10:22	202	41:11	25
10:23	202	42:2	27, 74, 115
14:36	47	42:5-6	36, 46
15:10	66		
15:29	64, 123	Psalms	
17:11	202	7:9	142
18:14	44	7:11	142
23:12	94	8:3-4	43
23:13	94	8:4	25
		11:7	142, 148
1 Kings		14:3	145
3:9	106	16:11	87, 105
8:27	34, 84	18:13	162
		18:30	142
2 Kings		19:7	107, 142
18:7	44	19:9	154
17:7-8	144	23:2	75
20:5-6	66	23:4	44
		25:10	164
1 Chronicles		27:13	164, 177
29:11	34, 115	27:14	124
		29:3	162
2 Chronicles		33:5	142
16:9	95	33:11	63
30:9	163	34:8	175
		34:18	87
Esther		37:28	142
2:1	26	39:4	56
2:2	26	46:1	44
4:1	26	46:7	44
4:14	27	46:11	44
		50:7-15	28
Job		50:12	26
1:9-11	8	50:21	6, 18, 157
2:4-5	8	51:6	106
9:4	103	51:7	167
11:7-10	34	52:2	123
12:13	106	66:18	46
14:5	57	68:5	45
15:15	133	68:5-6	46
25:5	133	71:12	44, 45
25:6	134	71:17	2
26:7	34	73:28	44
26:11	34	78:40	67
26:14	34, 94	84:11	175
28:24	95	86:15	164, 184
34:12	153	89:1	125
36:36	53	89:5	125
37:4-5	162	89:8	125
37:16	94	89:24	126
38:1	46	89:34	123
38:1-18	98	90:1-17	58

90:1-2	56		16:4	117
90:2	24, 58		21:1	115
90:4	55		21:15	155
90:12	2, 57, 59		30:3	134
92:15	153			
95:3-5	34		Ecclesiastes	
97:2	153		3:11	96, 104, 117
97:9	34			
102:25	23		Isaiah	
102:25-26	62		1:18	167
102:25-28	68		6:1	34, 36
102:27	24, 62		6:1-8	138
102:28	69		6:2	37, 135
103:8	163		6:2-3	34
103:13	67		6:3	133, 135
103:17	67		6:5	35, 36, 37, 123, 133
103:19	115		6:8	139
104:5	23		11:2	107
104:24	23, 103		14:13	8
105:8	123		14:27	27
107:1	177		26:4	57
111:10	107		28:17	154
115	18		30:18	157, 162
115:3	19, 114, 118		33:14	137
115:4	23		38:1-6	66
115:8	23		40:8	64
119:47	176		40:22	35
119:105	96		40:28	43, 53
119:168	175, 176, 178		42:16	106
130:3-4	144		44:6	24
135:6	115		45:4	95
136:1	183		45:7	116
138:6	35		46:9	202, 214
138:8	63		46:9-10	94
139:1-18	48		46:10	63
139:7	34, 46		48:12	24
139:7-10	84		48:18	106, 176
139:7-18	88		49:6	27, 144
139:16	57, 95		54:5	167
139:17	49		54:8	67
145:3	34		55:8	124
145:9	176		55:8-9	34, 176
147:5	74, 94, 98, 103		55:9	38
			57:15	36, 43, 55
Proverbs			59:2	86, 167
1:7	104		61:8	155
2:6	106		62:5	67
3:6	106		64:6	144, 193
3:19	103		65:16	163
9:6	105		66:1-2	84
9:7-12	108			
9:10	104, 109, 136		Jeremiah	
9:17	105		10:10	55
11:2	107		10:12	103
12:2	123		23:23-24	46, 84
15:3	88		23:24	34

29:7	177	Habakkuk	
29:10	124	1:12	134
29:11	124, 177	Zephaniah	
29:13	47	3:14-20	188
31:3	184	3:17	187
32:17	74, 78		

Lamentations
- 3:22-23   126, 163, 168
- 3:37   117

Zechariah
- 9:14   162

Ezekiel
- 18:20   157
- 18:25   155
- 24:14   64
- 28:17   8
- 33:11   157
- 34:11   46
- 34:15   46

Malachi
- 3:6   63, 68

Matthew
- 1:23   44
- 5:7   164
- 5:45   176
- 5:48   142
- 6:13   125
- 6:26   42
- 8:14-15   10
- 10:16-33   214
- 10:29   117
- 10:30   95
- 10:32-33   117, 215
- 10:33   204
- 11:18-19   95
- 11:21   95
- 13:35   63
- 14:13   75
- 14:15   75
- 14:16   75
- 14:20   10, 75
- 15:32   76
- 15:33   76
- 15:34   76
- 15:37   76
- 16:14   11
- 16:15-18   11
- 16:22-23   13
- 16:23   14
- 18:7-9   105
- 19:26   74
- 22:37   113
- 25:32   157
- 25:34   63
- 26:58   47
- 28:18   112
- 28:20   45, 86

Daniel
- 2:20   103
- 2:21   106
- 4:17   115
- 4:28-37   118
- 4:35   74, 115
- 5:23   115
- 7:9   24, 53
- 7:13   24
- 7:22   24
- 10:15-17   35

Hosea
- 1:2   165
- 3:2   166
- 3:3   166

Joel
- 2:13   163

Obadiah
- 1:15   85
- 1:18   85

Micah
- 6:8   176
- 7:18   164

Nahum
- 1:7   177

Jonah
- 3:4   66
- 3:10   66
- 4:11   66

Mark
- 6:34   75, 164
- 9:14-29   78
- 9:18   79
- 9:22   73
- 9:23   73

9:24	73	3:22-24	145
9:29	79	3:23	162, 167
10:18	173	3:23-24	195
12:30	96	3:26	65, 156
14:21	114	5:8	167, 186, 189, 196
15:31-32	202	5:9	157
		5:20	193
Luke		6:1-2	195
1:37	74	6:23	57, 155, 162, 192
3:22	186	8:4	107
5:8	35	8:18	104
6:36	164	8:28	105, 114
7:35	104	8:29	117
11:2	47	8:38-39	185
12:6	42	9:11	116
13:32	113	9:17	116
15:11-32	196	9:18	116
15:20	197	9:20	116
18:19	145	10:13	117
23:34	196	11:6	198
23:41	144	11:33	104, 108
		11:33-36	93
John		11:36	24
1:3	24, 53	12:2	96, 106
1:14	36, 44	12:19	156
3:16	185	13:1	112, 115
3:29	167	15:13	127
5:26	24	16:27	104
6:8	75		
6:44	116	1 Corinthians	
8:44	123	1:18	204, 205
12:27	114	1:24	107
14:26	105, 107	2:7	105
16:7	45	2:7-9	93
17:5	63	2:10-11	93
17:24	54	6:19	136
21:25	93	8:6	24
		10:13	124, 125
Acts		14:33	87
1:8	74	15:10	196
2:4	45		
4:13	45	2 Corinthians	
7:48	84	1:20	64, 123
9:4	135	5:21	144
9:9	135	10:5	97
9:25	76	12:7-10	105
17:24	23		
17:25	23, 28	Galatians	
17:27	48, 84	1:6	203
20:27	15	1:7	203
		1:10	204
Romans		2:20	186
1:18	192	5:11	205
1:20	74, 154	6:15	195
3:5	144		
3:10	145, 173		

Ephesians	
1:4	54, 63, 117
1:11	63, 116
2:1-10	198
2:4	167, 186
2:5	167
2:8-9	194
2:9	137
3:9	63
3:10	104
3:11	63
3:20	74
4:1	137
4:6	43
4:18	86
4:19	46
4:30	67
5:25-27	167

Philippians
1:6	123
2:7	36, 44
2:13	107

Colossians
1:16	24, 53, 167
1:17	24, 84
1:29	107
2:9-10	87
3:9	123
3:25	155

1 Thessalonians
1:10	157
5:9	157
5:24	126

2 Thessalonians
1:8	157
3:1-5	128
3:4	129

1 Timothy
4:4	175
6:16	34

2 Timothy
2:13	125, 128, 167
2:15	107
2:19	63
2:23-26	205
3:12	204

Titus
3:3-7	168
3:5	162

Hebrews
1:12	62
2:17	167
4:13	95
4:16	136, 164
6:17	63
6:19	177
9:27-28	158
10:10	137
11:6	24
11:25-26	105
12:2	117, 144, 167
12:14	134
12:29	136
13:8	62

James
1:5-6	106
1:12-18	178
1:13	125
1:14	178
1:17	63, 175, 178
2:10	155
2:13	164
3:13	107
4:8	47
4:14	56
4:15	56
5:11	164

1 Peter
1:3	162
1:10-12	194
1:14	137
1:16	137
1:19	145, 167
2:9	134
2:20	63
2:22	144
3:15	205

2 Peter
1:3	104
2:4	8
3:8	55, 124
3:9	124, 164
3:18	96

1 John
1:5	93
1:9	126, 157, 196
3:1	186, 204
3:5	144
3:20	94
4:7	183
4:8	183

4:16	184	7:11	135
4:19	183	12:10	184
5:3	176	12:11	185
		13:8	54, 63, 117
Jude		16:7	155
1:24-25	55	19:7-9	167
		19:10	134
Revelation		19:11	123
1:8	74	21:2	167
1:17	133	21:3	45
1:17-18	24	21:3-4	177
2-3	87	21:8	192
4:4	135	21:9	167
4:8	34, 133	21:22	45
4:10	135	21:23	45
4:11	23, 135	22:9	135

For more books, sermons, posts, articles, and resources, visit

TRAVISAGNEW.ORG

Made in the USA
Columbia, SC
28 May 2022